T0322320

THE COMPLETE
BAKING
AIR FRYER
COOKBOOK

THE COMPLETE BAKING AIR FRYER COOKBOOK

75 baking recipes perfect for your air fryer

CONTENTS

A GUIDE TO AIR FRYERS

TYPES OF AIR FRYER

There are lots of different air fryers available. The recipes in this book are based on an air fryer with a 5.7-litre capacity basket, which will fit a standard 20cm (8in) tin or ovenproof dish. Where a tin isn't required, the recipe can be baked in any size air fryer (the size of the basket will just affect the number of batches needed to cook the full recipe). If you have an air fryer with a small capacity, recipes can be halved to accommodate a smaller tin; as a general rule, reduce the baking time by one-third, then check the bake.

HOW AIR FRYERS WORK

It's good to understand how air fryers work, so that you can troubleshoot any baking hiccups. They have an electrical element at the top, and a fan that pushes the heat around a basket, in which the food sits. Place bakes on the rack provided, as this allows heat to circulate underneath them. Often a bake may look cooked and brown on top, but still need time to cook through from underneath where the heat is more gentle. Flipping is recommended for some bakes, while some are cooked at a higher heat initially to ensure the bake rises and colours, before decreasing the temperature to ensure thorough cooking.

SETTINGS

Most air fryers have multiple cooking settings. Use the bake setting unless the recipe states otherwise. Temperatures are the same as they would be if you were baking in a conventional oven, but some things will cook more quickly,

especially if they have a high fat content. Dense bakes, such as loaf cakes, however, take a similar amount of time. As an air fryer can heat up within minutes, this dramatically reduces energy usage and makes for a very convenient way to bake. The re-heat setting is great for warming bakes just before serving.

BAKING IN A TIN

Consider the size of your air fryer before buying tins to fit. You can use all ovenproof dishes. Metal tins conduct heat quickly and retain that heat, so are good for getting a golden, crisp crust. Silicone is great for bakes that need a non-stick surface. If a recipe says to grease a tin, you can use soft butter, oil, or an oil spray. If the recipe also advises lining, cut a piece of baking parchment to the size of the base, then another for the sides. Trim any excess as it may catch on the element or blow around and damage your bake.

BAKING DIRECTLY IN THE BASKET

Some recipes require you place the bake directly into the air fryer basket. Make sure you have the rack in the basket to allow the air to circulate for even baking. All air fryer racks have a non-stick coating, but giving them a light spray with oil can help ensure no sticking. Some recipes, such as cookies, call for the basket to be lined to prevent the bakes melting through the gaps. Cut a piece of baking parchment to the width of the rack, and fold any excess under to prevent the paper from being blown about during baking.

REMOVING BAKES FROM THE BASKET

Wearing oven gloves (mitts) is the safest way to remove anything from most air fryers. There are also many bakes that need to cool and set, such as cookies or pastries. The easiest way to do this without any casualties, is to remove the basket from the fryer and set it on a wire rack to cool. Once the bakes have cooled to room temperature, use a spatula or your hands to gently lift them out.

BAKING IN BATCHES

Some recipes, such as cookies, will require baking in batches due to the lack of space in the air fryer. They take up lots of surface area and need to be spaced out while baking to stop them from sticking to one another. Cookies, biscuits, and pastry are always best chilled before baking because of their high fat content, so it is best to store batches in the fridge until you're ready to bake them.

FREEZING

As a general rule, all cookies, biscuits, and pastries can be frozen while raw. This is super-handy if you want to make a recipe, but don't want the full quantity at once, or want to prepare ahead for the future. Open-freeze cookies or pastries on a lined baking tray, then transfer to an airtight container (this prevents them from sticking together). To bake from frozen, increase the time slightly and keep checking until cooked. Alternatively, leave to thaw at room temperature and bake as the recipe suggests.

5 BEST BAKES TO COOK IN THE AIR FRYER

1 **GOOEY BROWNIES**

2 **SWEET AND SAVOURY PASTRIES**

3 **COOKIES**

4 **MUFFINS AND CAKES**

5 **SWEET BUNS**

BREAKFAST BAKES

Whether you opt for a sweet Danish, muffin, or pancake with your morning coffee or a nourishing savoury morsel, this chapter is full of simple breakfast ideas for your air fryer, as well as lots of options for making ahead to fill your freezer ready for those busy mornings.

BANANA & COFFEE MUFFINS

180g (generous ¾ cup) plain yogurt
140ml (scant ⅔ cup) vegetable oil
2 large (US extra large) eggs
150g (¾ cup) soft light brown sugar
3 small ripe bananas, mashed with
   some chunks left
1 tsp coffee essence
75g (¾ cup) pecan halves,
   roughly chopped
150g (1 cup plus 2 tbsp) self-raising
   (self-rising) flour
150g (1 cup plus 2 tbsp) wholemeal
   (wholewheat) flour
1 tbsp instant coffee powder
1 tsp baking powder
½ tsp salt

CRUMBLE TOPPING:
50g (3½ tbsp) salted butter,
   cold and cubed
50g (6 tbsp) plain (all-purpose) flour
25g (2 tbsp) soft brown sugar
25g (¼ cup) pecan halves,
   roughly chopped
1 tsp instant coffee powder

1 Start by making the crumble topping. Place the cubed butter in a bowl with the flour, and rub between your fingers until you have a chunky crumble. Stir through the sugar, chopped pecans, and instant coffee. Set aside.
2 Combine the yogurt, oil, eggs, and sugar in a large bowl, and whisk until the sugar has dissolved. Add the mashed bananas, coffee essence, and chopped pecans, and fold through the mix. Sift the remaining dry ingredients into the bowl and fold again until everything is fully incorporated.
3 Preheat the air fryer to 160°C/325°F for 3 minutes.
4 Place 12 silicone muffin cases directly into the air fryer basket (or work in batches if needed), then fill each case about four-fifths full with batter.

5 Top generously with the crumble mixture.
6 Bake at 160°C/325°F for 25 minutes, then leave to cool on a wire rack.

KEEP IT Store for up to 5 days in an airtight container or freeze for up to 6 weeks.

Prep + cook time
40 minutes
Makes 12

PISTACHIO PAIN AU RAISIN

100g (⅔ cup) raisins, soaked in
    boiling water
320g (11oz) sheet of puff pastry
100g (3½oz) pistachios, finely
    chopped
1 egg, beaten
100g (3½oz) apricot jam

PASTRY CREAM:
2 egg yolks
2 tbsp cornflour (cornstarch)
50g (¼ cup) caster (superfine) sugar
1 tsp vanilla paste
200ml (scant 1 cup) full-fat
    (whole) milk

1 For the pastry cream, whisk the yolks, cornflour, sugar, and vanilla in a large heatproof bowl until the mixture starts to loosen.
2 Heat the milk in a wide saucepan over a medium heat until starting to steam. Pour one-third into the yolk mixture, and whisk until combined. Stir in the rest of the hot milk and pour everything back into the pan over the heat.
3 Whisk the custard until it is really thick, then remove from the heat and beat well.
4 Pour the custard onto a clean baking tray (to help it to cool quickly), and cover with clingfilm to stop a skin from forming. Let cool.
5 Drain the soaked raisins well in a sieve. Set aside.
6 Unroll the pastry, keeping it on the paper. Spread the cooled pastry cream evenly over the pastry.
7 Sprinkle with the raisins and three-quarters of the pistachios.

8 Using the edge of the paper, roll the pastry tightly into a swirl from one of the short ends. Wrap in the paper and chill for 30 minutes.
9 Preheat the air fryer to 160°C/325°F for 3 minutes and line the basket with baking parchment.
10 Cut the roll into eight pieces, place on a lined tray, and brush with egg. Cook in batches (keep the other pastries in the fridge) in the lined air fryer basket for 25 minutes at 160°C/325°F. Cool on a wire rack.
11 Heat the apricot jam for 30 seconds in a microwave to loosen it, then brush it over the pastries. Top with the remaining pistachios.

KEEP IT Best eaten fresh, but will keep for 2 days in an airtight container. Reheat for 2 minutes in the air fryer.

**Prep + cook time
40 minutes, plus chilling
Makes 8**

MAPLE SYRUP PANCAKES

200g (1½ cups) plain (all-purpose) flour
½ tsp baking powder
½ tsp bicarbonate of soda (baking soda)
¼ tsp fine salt
1 large (US extra large) egg
60ml (4 tbsp) maple syrup
300g (1½ cups) plain yogurt or kefir
20g (1½ tbsp) unsalted butter, melted
to serve: Greek yogurt, berries, and maple syrup

1 Combine all the dry ingredients in a large mixing bowl. Whisk the egg, maple syrup, and yogurt in another. Pour the combined wet ingredients into the dry ingredients, and whisk until you have a smooth batter. Mix through the melted butter, and leave the batter to rest for 10 minutes or up to 1 hour.
2 Preheat the air fryer to 180°C/350°F for 3 minutes.
3 Fill ten greased 10cm (4in) tart moulds roughly 1cm (½in) deep with pancake batter, then place in the air fryer basket and bake for 5 minutes at 180°C/350°F (you may need to do this in batches).

4 Remove the pancakes from the moulds, flip them over, and return to the fryer basket (without their moulds) for another 3 minutes.
5 Once all your pancakes are baked, stack them up and serve with yogurt, berries, and maple syrup.

**Prep + cook time
30 minutes
Makes 10**

OATY BLUEBERRY MUFFINS

200g (1 cup) plain yogurt

140ml (scant ⅔ cup) vegetable oil

45ml (3 tbsp) maple syrup

2 large (US extra large) eggs

100g (½ cup) soft light brown sugar, plus 1 tbsp for topping

200g (1½ cups) self-raising (self-rising) flour

50g (½ cup) rolled (old-fashioned) oats, plus 2 tbsp for topping

1 tsp ground cinnamon

1 tsp baking powder

½ tsp salt

150g (1¼ cups) fresh blueberries or 150g (¾ cup) frozen blueberries

2 tbsp pumpkin seeds, plus 2 tbsp for topping

1 Combine all the wet ingredients with the sugar in a bowl, and whisk until the sugar dissolves.

2 Add all the dry ingredients and mix until fully incorporated. Fold through the blueberries and pumpkin seeds.

3 Make the topping by mixing 1 tablespoon brown sugar with 2 tablespoons oats and 2 tablespoons pumpkin seeds in a bowl.

4 Preheat the air fryer to 160°C/325°F for 3 minutes.

5 Place 8 silicone muffin cases (lined with paper, if you like) directly into the air fryer basket (or work in batches if needed), then fill each case about four-fifths full with batter.

6 Sprinkle with the crunchy topping.

7 Bake at 160°C/325°F for 25 minutes, then leave to cool on a wire rack.

KEEP IT Store for up to 5 days in an airtight container, or freeze for up to 6 weeks.

**Prep + cook time
40 minutes
Makes 8**

APRICOT & ALMOND DANISHES

400g (14oz) can apricot halves
320g (11oz) sheet of puff pastry
1 tbsp milk
30g (⅓ cup) flaked (slivered)
   almonds
150g (5¼oz) apricot jam
to serve: icing (confectioners') sugar

FRANGIPANE:
50g (3½ tbsp) salted butter, softened
50g (¼ cup) golden caster
   (superfine) sugar
80g (¾ cup) ground almonds
1 large (US extra large) egg
1 tsp vanilla paste
25g (3 tbsp) plain (all-purpose) flour

TIP Heat the pastries for 1 minute at 160°C/325°F before serving for that just-baked warm taste!

1 Start by making the frangipane. In a mixing bowl, beat the butter and sugar with a wooden spoon for 3–5 minutes. Add the almonds, egg, and vanilla, and stir until combined. Fold in the flour.
2 Drain the apricots over a sieve and discard the syrup. Slice each apricot half into thirds; set aside.
3 Unroll the sheet of puff pastry and cut it into six 10cm (4in) squares (or a size to suit your air fryer).
4 Score a 2cm (¾in) border around the edge of each square, then place one-sixth of the frangipane in the centre of each square. Gently spread the mixture out to fill the inner square.
5 Place the sliced apricots in rows on top of the frangipane. Nestle them close to each other, as they will shrink when baking.
6 Preheat the air fryer to 200°C/400°F for 3 minutes.
7 Brush each pastry edge with milk.

8 Using a spatula, place 2–4 pastries in the air fryer basket. Bake for 5 minutes at 200°C/400°F, then 15 minutes at 160°C/325°F. Cool on a wire rack. Repeat to cook all the pastries.
9 Place the flaked almonds in a single layer in a heatproof dish. Toast for 4–6 minutes at 160°C/325°F. Check and stir often, as they can burn quickly.
10 Heat the apricot jam in a small saucepan over a low heat for 2–3 minutes, then brush over the pastries. Place the toasted almonds around the edge.
11 Dust with icing sugar and serve fresh.

KEEP IT Make ahead to the end of step 5, cover, and leave in the fridge overnight. Or freeze for 6 weeks, separated by greaseproof paper. Defrost for 20 minutes before baking.

Prep + cook time
45 minutes
Makes 6

STRAWBERRY & YOGURT SHORTCAKES

50ml (3½ tbsp) milk, plus extra
    for brushing
juice of ½ lemon
150g (1 cup plus 2 tbsp) plain
    (all-purpose) flour, plus extra
    for dusting
40g (3¼ tbsp) golden caster
    (superfine) sugar, plus 1 tbsp
    for topping
½ tsp baking powder
50g (3½ tbsp) cold butter
1 egg, beaten

TOPPING:
200g (7oz) strawberries, hulled
    and sliced
1 tbsp honey, plus extra to serve
juice of ½ lemon
160g (¾ cup) Greek yogurt
1 tsp vanilla paste

1 Start by combining the milk with the lemon juice, and set aside. Combine the flour, sugar, and baking powder in a bowl, then grate the cold butter into the bowl, using the largest side on a box grater.

2 Pour the milk and lemon mixture into the bowl along with the beaten egg.

3 Using your hand in a claw shape, combine the mixture into a rough dough until everything is combined but there are still visible pieces of butter.

4 Tip the dough out onto a lightly floured surface. Bring it together into a rectangle about 2.5cm (1in) thick.

5 Roll the dough into a 20 x 10cm (8 x 4in) rectangle. Fold it in half, rotate it 90°, then roll out again to a 20 x 10cm (8 x 4in) rectangle. Fold in half again and pat with your hands to seal the top layer to the bottom layer.

6 Cut the dough in half to make two rectangular shortcakes. Brush with milk and sprinkle with golden caster sugar.

7 Preheat the air fryer to 180°C/350°F for 3 minutes.

8 Place the shortcakes directly into the basket and bake for 16 minutes.

9 For the topping, combine the strawberries with the honey and lemon juice in a bowl, and set aside. Combine the Greek yogurt and vanilla paste in a mixing bowl, and whisk for 2 minutes.

10 Leave the shortcakes to cool for 5–10 minutes.

11 To serve, cut open the shortcakes, top with generous dollops of yogurt, some macerated strawberries, and an extra drizzle of honey.

Prep + cook time
30 minutes
Makes 2

SEEDED BREAKFAST BAGELS

1 tsp active dried yeast
150ml (⅔ cup) lukewarm water
250g (1¾ cups) strong white
   bread flour, plus extra for dusting
1 tbsp caster (superfine) sugar
½ tsp sea salt
1 tsp bicarbonate of soda
   (baking soda)
2 tbsp sesame, nigella, poppy,
   or sunflower seeds
flaked sea salt
vegetable oil cooking spray

FILLING SUGGESTIONS:
smoked salmon, cream cheese,
   pickles, and salad
peanut butter and jam (jelly)
fried egg, hash brown, and sausage

1 Sprinkle the yeast over the warm water and stir to combine. Set aside for a couple of minutes until the yeast begins to foam. Spray five small squares of baking parchment with cooking oil spray. Set aside.
2 Place the flour, sugar, and salt in a large bowl. Stir briefly, so the sugar and salt are distributed, then add the yeasted water. Bring it together with a wooden spoon until you have a shaggy dough.
3 Tip the dough out onto a floured surface and knead for 5–8 minutes until you have a smooth, bouncy dough. Alternatively, use a stand mixer with a dough hook attachment.
4 Divide the dough into five pieces, and roll each piece into a ball. Using your hand like a claw, roll it in circular motions, pressing gently with your palm. Press a hole into the centre of each ball with your index finger; twirl it around your finger to create the bagel shape.

5 Place each bagel on an oiled square of parchment on a baking tray, spray lightly with oil, and cover with clingfilm. Leave to prove in a warm place for 30 minutes–1 hour, or until doubled in size.
6 Bring a large pan of water to the boil and add the bicarbonate of soda. Tip one bagel at a time into the boiling water (use the paper to tip them in). Boil for 30 seconds on each side. Drain on a wire rack.
7 Preheat the air fryer to 180°C/350°F for 3 minutes.
8 Spray the bagels with oil, then sprinkle with seeds and flaked sea salt. Place in the air fryer basket and bake for 12 minutes at 180°C/350°F until golden.
9 Transfer to a wire rack and cool for 10 minutes.

KEEP IT Store in an airtight container for up to 5 days.

Prep + cook time
1 hour 30 minutes
Makes 5

CHEESY BEAN PARCELS

320g (11oz) sheet of puff pastry
50g (scant ½ cup) pre-grated mozzarella
50g (scant ½ cup) grated cheddar
1 egg, beaten

BAKED BEANS:
1 shallot, finely diced
2 tbsp olive oil
400g (14oz) can haricot beans, drained
400g (14oz) can chopped tomatoes
½ tsp smoked paprika
½ tsp garlic powder
1 tbsp Marmite
1 tbsp soft light brown sugar
½ tsp salt
to serve: ketchup (optional)

TIP You will have a portion of beans left! Keep these for a delicious breakfast during the week.

1 Preheat the air fryer to 180°C/350°F for 3 minutes.
2 For the beans, put the diced shallot inside a 1-litre (4-cup) silicone liner or heatproof dish, drizzle with the olive oil, and season. Stir to coat, then roast for 8 minutes at 180°C/350°F.
3 Add the remaining baked beans ingredients and 3½ tablespoons water, season with freshly ground black pepper, and combine. Bake at 180°C/350°F for 20 minutes, stir, then bake for a further 30 minutes.
4 Spread the baked beans onto a clean baking tray to help them cool quickly.
5 Unroll the pastry and cut vertically into three strips. Place two generous spoons of cooled beans on the top half of each strip, leaving a 2cm (¾in) gap around the sides. Top with one-quarter of the cheeses.
6 Brush the edges of the pastry with beaten egg, then fold the bottom half over to make a parcel.

7 Use the sides of your hands to cup around the filling, pushing down gently to seal the pastry.
8 Trim the edges, then use a fork to crimp the sealed sides. Brush with egg, then cut a 2cm (¾in) slit in the centre of the pastry (for steam to escape). Sprinkle with the remaining cheese.
9 Place in the fridge for 20 minutes to firm up.
10 Preheat the air fryer to 200°C/400°F for 3 minutes.
11 Place them directly into the basket and bake for 10 minutes at 200°C/400°F, then for 15 minutes at 160°C/325°F. Let cool slightly before serving.

KEEP IT Make to the end of step 8, cover, and keep in the fridge overnight. Or freeze for 6 weeks, separated by greaseproof paper. Defrost for 30 minutes prior to baking.

**Prep + cook time
1 hour 30 minutes,
plus chilling
Makes 3**

SHAKSHUKA PASTRY CUPS

1 tbsp finely chopped coriander (cilantro) stalks
1 garlic clove, finely chopped
½ tsp smoked paprika
1 tsp ground cumin
1 tsp chilli flakes
½ tsp salt
1 tbsp olive oil, plus extra for drizzling
400g (14oz) can chopped tomatoes
½ x 320g (11oz) sheet of puff pastry
4 eggs
to serve: Greek yogurt and coriander leaves

1 Preheat the air fryer to 180°C/350°F for 3 minutes.

2 Start by making the spiced tomato sauce. Add the coriander stalks, garlic, spices, salt, a few grinds of black pepper, and the oil to a heatproof dish or silicone tray. Roast at 180°C/350°F for 3 minutes.

3 Pour in the chopped tomatoes, combine, and roast for a further 15 minutes. Remove from the air fryer and set aside to cool.

4 Cut four 10cm (4in) squares of pastry. Place each piece of pastry into a metal pudding tin, using your thumbs to push the pastry up the sides of the tin to create a cup.

5 Fill each cup with a tablespoon of the cooled tomato sauce.

6 Crack an egg into each cup, then top gently with another tablespoon of sauce. Season and drizzle with olive oil.

7 Preheat the air fryer to 180°C/350°F for 3 minutes.

8 Bake the shakshuka cups for 16 minutes at 180°C/350°F for a runny yolk centre, or 20 minutes for a hard yolk.

9 Leave to cool for 5 minutes before removing from the tins, then serve warm with a dollop of Greek yogurt and a few coriander leaves.

**Prep + cook time
30 minutes
Makes 4**

FRITTATA MUFFINS (GLUTEN-FREE)

6 large (US extra large) eggs
100ml (⅓ cup) milk
2 tbsp snipped chives
½ tsp garlic powder
1 tsp salt
to serve: ketchup (optional)

SUPER GREENS AND FETA FILLING:
1 handful of spinach
1 small bunch of dill, thick stalks
   removed
1 small bunch of coriander (cilantro),
   thick stalks removed
100g (3½oz) feta, crumbled

ROASTED VEG FILLING:
1 (bell) pepper, diced
1 courgette (zucchini), diced
50g (⅓ cup) frozen sweetcorn
1 tsp olive oil
½ tsp chilli flakes
½ tsp salt

BACON AND CHEDDAR FILLING:
200g (7oz) bacon lardons
100g (scant 1 cup) grated cheddar

1 Make your choice of filling. For the super greens and feta filling, roughly chop the spinach and herbs. Add to a small food processor or blender with 1 tablespoon water, and blitz until it resembles a chunky pesto. Stir through the crumbled feta, and season with black pepper.

2 For the roasted veg filling, preheat the air fryer to 200°C/400°F for 3 minutes. Combine the ingredients in a heatproof dish, and roast for 20 minutes at 200°C/400°F until charred.

3 For the bacon and cheddar filling, preheat the air fryer to 200°C/400°F for 3 minutes. Place the lardons directly into the air fryer, and cook at 200°C/400°F for 8 minutes, or until crispy. Leave to cool on a piece of kitchen towel, then combine with the grated cheese and some black pepper.

4 To make the frittata, combine the eggs, milk, chives, garlic powder, salt, and plenty of black pepper in a large bowl. Whisk until silky, then pour the mixture into a jug.

5 Preheat the air fryer to 180°C/350°F for 3 minutes.

6 Place 12 silicone muffin cases directly into the air fryer basket (or cook in batches), then fill each case three-quarters full with your chosen filling. Top up each case with the egg, leaving 5mm (¼in) space for the muffins to rise.

7 Bake for 12 minutes at 180°C/350°F; if they're still very wobbly, bake for a further 3 minutes.

8 Let cool in the cases for 5 minutes before removing.

KEEP IT Store for up to 3 days in an airtight container in the fridge.

Prep + cook time
30 minutes
Makes 12

SNACKS

When you are in need of a little pick-me-up, the air fryer is your friend. The hot circulating air creates the crispest pastry twists and seedy bagel straws. For a more substantial snack to please a crowd, try Mini Pizzas 3 Ways (see p44) or Kimchi & Cheese Toasties (see p43).

EVERYTHING BAGEL STRAWS

320g (11oz) sheet of puff pastry
1 egg, beaten

EVERYTHING BAGEL MIX:
2 tbsp white sesame seeds
1 tbsp black sesame seeds
1 tbsp poppy seeds
½ tsp garlic powder
½ tsp onion powder
1 tsp salt
1 tsp coarse black pepper

SOUR CREAM DIP:
150g (5¼oz) sour cream
25g (¾oz) pickles of your choice,
    finely diced (onion, gherkin,
    capers, etc.)
1 tsp English (hot) mustard
1 tbsp snipped chives

1 Combine all the everything bagel mix ingredients in a small bowl, then set aside.
2 Unroll the pastry sheet, keeping it on the paper, and brush with the beaten egg. Sprinkle the whole sheet in the seed mix; you want the whole surface to be covered, but you may not need it all.
3 Cut the pastry in half crossways, then cut both pieces into 2.5cm (1in) thick strips.
4 Preheat the air fryer to 180°C/350°F for 3 minutes.
5 Working in batches, place the strips directly into the air fryer basket, seeded-side up, leaving a 2cm (¾in) gap between each strip, as they will double in size. Bake at 180°C/350°F for 10 minutes.

6 While the straws are baking, combine the dip ingredients and season to taste.
7 Serve the straws with the dip. They are best served fresh, but can be reheated just before serving, if necessary.

TIP You can save any remaining seed mix to top soups, salads, or eggs.

**Prep + cook time
30 minutes
Makes 32**

PADRÓN PEPPER POPPERS

180g (6½oz) fresh padrón peppers
300g (1⅓ cups) cream cheese
1 large (US extra large) egg, beaten
30g (4 tbsp) plain (all-purpose) flour
1 tsp garlic powder
60g (1½ cups) panko breadcrumbs
50g (¾ cup) finely grated Parmesan
vegetable or olive oil cooking spray

1 Prepare the padrón peppers. Wash and dry them, then slice off the tops and carefully remove the inner stems.

2 Fill a piping (pastry) bag with the cream cheese (or use a sandwich bag and snip the corner off). Fill each padrón pepper with cream cheese, then set aside while you prepare the coating.

3 Place the beaten egg in a wide-based bowl. Mix the flour with the garlic powder in another bowl and season with salt and pepper. Put the panko breadcrumbs and grated Parmesan in a third bowl.

4 Working in batches, dust the stuffed peppers lightly in flour, then coat in the egg, then roll in the panko breadcrumb and cheese mixture.

5 Preheat the air fryer to 180°C/350°F for 3 minutes.

6 Place the peppers directly into the preheated air fryer basket, spray with oil, and bake at 180°C/350°F for 12 minutes.

7 Serve straight away.

SERVE IT Serve hot with a bowl of sweet chilli sauce for dipping or a drizzle of hot honey and plenty of flaked sea salt.

**Prep + cook time
30 minutes
Makes 16**

CHEDDAR SCONES

250g (scant 2 cups) plain (all-purpose) flour, plus extra for dusting
1 tsp baking powder
70g (5 tbsp) unsalted butter, cold
200g (scant 2 cups) grated cheddar
100ml (⅓ cup) full-fat (whole) milk, plus extra for brushing
1 tsp English (hot) mustard
1 tsp sea salt
1 tsp ground black pepper

1 Place the plain flour and baking powder in a medium mixing bowl, then grate in the cold butter using the largest side of a box grater.
2 Rub the butter into the flour using your fingertips until the mix resembles fine breadcrumbs. Stir through 150g (scant 1½ cups) grated cheddar.
3 Whisk the milk, mustard, salt, and pepper together, then pour into the flour mix. Using a spoon, combine until it resembles a shaggy dough. Tip out the dough onto a lightly floured work surface.
4 Knead gently until the dough just comes together, then shape into a circle about 5cm (2in) thick. Cut it into six triangles. Place on a lined tray, cover, and chill for at least 30 minutes (or up to overnight).

5 Preheat the air fryer to 200°C/400°F for 3 minutes.
6 Brush each scone with milk, then sprinkle with the remaining cheese.
7 Place directly into the air fryer basket and bake for 15 minutes at 200°C/400°F. Allow to cool before serving.

SERVE IT Cut them open and serve with salted butter, ham, mustard, and pickles.

Prep + cook time
45 minutes, plus chilling
Makes 6

MINI SAVOURY GALETTES

400g (3 cups) wholemeal (wholewheat) flour, plus extra for dusting
1 tbsp nigella seeds
1 tsp salt
200g (1¾ sticks) cold butter
2 tbsp cold water
seasonal veggies of your choice, such as asparagus
drizzle of olive oil
herbs of your choice, such as parsley, basil, tarragon, or chives
1 egg, beaten
to serve: pickled red onion

FILLING:
250g (1 cup) ricotta
1 large (US extra large) egg
40g (½ cup) finely grated Parmesan, plus extra to serve
1 garlic clove

1 Place the flour in a large mixing bowl and combine with the nigella seeds and salt. Grate the cold butter into the bowl, using the largest side on a box grater. Add the cold water.
2 Using your fingertips, rub the butter into the flour. As the dough starts to clump, use your hand to bring it into a ball. Don't worry if there are still flecks of butter, you just want all the flour absorbed. Wrap in clingfilm and put in the fridge for 20 minutes.
3 Meanwhile, combine the filling ingredients in a bowl.
4 Prepare your chosen veggies as needed. If using any root vegetables, be sure to slice thinly or part-roast. Toss in olive oil, your chosen herbs, and some salt and pepper.
5 Cut the chilled dough into eight equal pieces and roll into rough balls.
6 On a floured surface, roll out into 15cm (6in) circles.

7 Divide the ricotta filling amongst the pastry circles. Spread the mixture out, but leave a 3cm (1¼in) border.
8 Layer the veggies on top, then fold in the edges of the pastry, pushing the corners to seal in the toppings. Brush the edges with egg. If the pastry has softened, transfer to a lined tray and chill for 30 minutes.
9 Preheat the air fryer to 180°C/350°F for 3 minutes.
10 Using a spatula, place the galettes directly into the basket. Bake at 180°C/350°F for 20 minutes until the pastry is golden and the base is crisp.
11 Cool for 5–10 minutes before serving topped with a grating of Parmesan and some pickled red onion.

KEEP IT Keep for 3 days in an airtight container in the fridge. Reheat in the air fryer.

Prep + cook time
1 hour, plus chilling
Makes 8

KIMCHI & CHEESE TOASTIES

30g (2 tbsp) salted butter, softened
4 large slices of bread (white or brown)
2 tsp hot sauce, plus extra to serve
2 tbsp kimchi
1 spring onion (scallion)
60g (2oz) mozzarella
2 tbsp sesame seeds

1 Butter each side of the bread. Trim off the crusts.
2 Spread 1 teaspoon hot sauce on two slices of the bread, then place 1 tablespoon kimchi in the centre of the slice, along with half the mozzarella, making sure to leave a 2cm (¾in) border around the edge of the slice.
3 Place a buttered piece of bread on top, and, using the sides of your hands, push down the border to seal the filling inside.
4 Place the sesame seeds on a plate, then push each side of the buttered parcels into the seeds until they are evenly coated. Cut a 1cm (½in) hole in the centre of the bread for the steam to escape as they bake.

5 Preheat the air fryer to 180°C/350°F for 3 minutes.
6 Place the parcels directly into the air fryer basket and bake for 8 minutes at 180°C/350°F. Flip the toast over, then bake for a further 3 minutes.
7 Leave to cool for 5 minutes before cutting in half and serving with extra hot sauce.

**Prep + cook time
30 minutes
Makes 2**

MINI PIZZAS 3 WAYS

200g (1½ cups) self-raising (self-rising) flour, plus extra for dusting
200g (1 cup) plain yogurt
½ tsp baking powder
1 tsp salt

TOPPINGS
100g (3½oz) basil and oregano passata (strained tomatoes) or fresh basil pesto
125g (4oz) ball of mozzarella, torn
125g (4oz) toppings of your choice

TIP For a tomato base: try adding bacon lardons, or alternatively go for marinated red peppers or sundried tomatoes, and finish with some basil leaves once cooked.

For a basil pesto base: try topping with thinly sliced courgette (zucchini), chilli flakes, and lemon zest, and finishing with shaved Parmesan once cooked.

1 Combine the flour, yogurt, baking powder, and salt in a bowl, and mix with a wooden spoon until fully combined. Once it starts to form a soft ball of dough, use your hand to bring it together. If it is still sticky, sprinkle in a little extra flour until you can handle the dough easily.

2 Scrape the dough out onto a lightly floured surface, and knead for 2 minutes to bring it together into a smooth ball. This isn't like a regular yeasted pizza dough, so it doesn't require lots of kneading. Place a clean tea towel over the dough.

3 Get all of your pizza toppings ready.

4 Preheat the air fryer to 200°C/400°F for 3 minutes.

5 Cut the dough into six pieces. On the floured work surface, use your hands to gently push out the dough into 10cm (4in) circles.

6 Dust off any excess flour, then top your pizzas with your chosen toppings and season with salt and black pepper. Gently transfer to the pre-heated air fryer using a flour-dusted spatula to place the pizzas directly onto the rack (the pizzas will increase in size, so be sure to leave a 2.5cm (1in) gap between them.

7 Cook at 200°C/400°F for 8–12 minutes, or until the base is crisp. Serve hot.

KEEP IT They will keep for 3 days in the fridge. Use the re-heat setting on the air fryer to warm them through, or serve cold.

Prep + cook time
30 minutes
Makes 6

ONE-BOWL YOGURT CAKES

200g (1 cup) plain yogurt
120ml (½ cup) vegetable oil
2 large (US extra large) eggs
150g (¾ cup) caster (superfine)
    sugar
1 tsp vanilla paste
grated zest of ½ lemon
180g (1⅓ cups) self-raising
    (self-rising) flour
1 tsp baking powder

1 Combine the yogurt, oil, eggs, sugar, vanilla, and lemon zest in a large mixing bowl, then sift in the flour and baking powder. Combine with a whisk until you have a smooth batter.
2 Place 12 silicone cupcake cases (lined with paper cases, if you like) into the air fryer basket. Using a cookie scoop or spoon, fill the cases three-quarters full.
3 Preheat the air fryer to 160°C/325°F for 3 minutes.

4 Bake at 160°C/325°F for 15 minutes.
5 Remove the basket from the air fryer and leave to cool for 5 minutes before lifting the cakes out.
6 Remove the cakes from the silicone cases when still slightly warm, then leave to cool fully on a wire rack.

TIP Store in an airtight container for up to 5 days.

**Prep + cook time
30 minutes
Makes 12**

47

BAKEWELL TWISTS WITH RASPBERRY JAM DIP

320g (11oz) sheet of puff pastry
50g (generous ½ cup) flaked
   (slivered) almonds
150g (1 cup) icing (confectioners')
   sugar
5 raspberries
juice of 1 lemon

FRANGIPANE:
50g (3½ tbsp) salted butter, softened
50g (¼ cup) caster (superfine) sugar
1 large (US extra large) egg
80g (¾ cup) ground almonds
1 tbsp milk, plus extra for brushing
1 tsp almond essence
25g (3 tbsp) plain (all-purpose) flour

RASPBERRY JAM DIP:
140g (5oz) frozen or fresh
   raspberries
60g (5 tbsp) caster (superfine) sugar
grated zest of 1 lemon

1 For the frangipane, beat the butter and sugar with a wooden spoon for 2–3 minutes. Add the egg, almonds, milk, and almond essence, and combine. Fold in the flour. Set aside.
2 Unroll the pastry sheet, keeping it on the paper. Using the back of a spoon, spread the frangipane across the pastry. Use the paper to help you fold the pastry in half lengthways. Wrap it in its paper and place on a baking tray. Chill for 20 minutes.
3 Preheat the air fryer to 180°C/350°F for 3 minutes.
4 Place the flaked almonds in a single layer in a heatproof dish. Toast for 2 minutes at 180°C/350°F. Stir, then bake for a further 2 minutes, or until golden brown. Set aside.
5 To make the jam dip, crush the raspberries in a bowl with the sugar and lemon zest, then transfer to a heatproof dish.

6 Cook for 10 minutes at 180°C/350°F. Stir, then cook for 5 minutes more. Set aside to cool.
7 Cut the chilled pastry crossways into 2.5cm (1in) thick strips. Twist each strip, then brush with milk.
8 Put the twists into the air fryer basket (in batches), leaving a 2cm (¾in) gap between them. Bake at 180°C/350°F for 12 minutes.
9 Sift the icing sugar into a large bowl. In a small bowl, crush the 5 raspberries with the back of a fork, and combine with the lemon juice. Add to the icing sugar, and mix well.
10 Place the twists on a wire rack. Brush with the raspberry icing while still warm, then sprinkle with the almonds before it sets. Serve with the dip! Best eaten on the same day.

Prep + cook time
45 minutes, plus chilling
Makes 12

TROPICAL FRUIT & COCONUT BARS (VEGAN & GLUTEN-FREE)

220g (7¾oz) dairy-free butter

60g (3 tbsp) golden syrup

100g (½ cup) soft light brown sugar

200g (2 cups) gluten-free rolled (old-fashioned) oats

80g (1 cup) desiccated (dried unsweetened) coconut

10g (1½ tbsp) poppy or chia seeds

80g (3oz) dried mango, chopped into small chunks

50g (2oz) dried pineapple, chopped into small chunks

1½ tsp salt

1 Preheat the air fryer to 180°C/350°F for 3 minutes.

2 Combine the butter, syrup, and sugar in a heatproof dish. Place in the air fryer for 4 minutes at 180°C/350°F. The mixture should be melted and starting to bubble.

3 Combine all the remaining dry ingredients in a large mixing bowl. Pour in the hot syrup, and stir with a spoon until all the oats are coated.

4 Pour the mixture into a 20cm (8in) lined brownie tin, then press down with the back of the spoon; the mix should be compact and even.

5 Place the tin into the air fryer basket and bake for 16 minutes at 180°C/350°F.

6 Leave to cool in the tin on a wire rack. Once cooled, turn out of the tin and cut into eight rectangles.

KEEP IT Will keep for up to 7 days in an airtight container.

**Prep + cook time
30 minutes
Makes 8**

PASTEL DE NATA

320g (11oz) sheet of puff pastry
1 tsp ground cinnamon,
   plus extra to decorate
plain (all-purpose) flour, for dusting
250ml (1 cup) vanilla custard

1 Unroll the puff pastry sheet, keeping it on the paper. Sprinkle the whole piece of pastry with ground cinnamon.
2 Taking one of the long edges, roll the pastry into a tight swirl.
3 Cut the pastry into eight pieces. On a lightly floured work surface, roll each piece of pastry into a 7.5–10cm (3–4in) circle.
4 Preheat the air fryer to 200°C/400°F for 3 minutes.
5 Place each circle of pastry into a metal pudding tin, gently pushing the pastry into the tin.

6 Fill each pastry case two-thirds full with custard, then place into the air fryer basket, and bake for 16 minutes at 200°C/400°F.
7 Leave to cool in the tins for 10 minutes before removing from the tins and serving warm with a dusting of cinnamon.

Prep + cook time
30 minutes
Makes 8

COOKIES & BROWNIES

The ease of the air fryer will take you
by surprise when it comes to baking
cookies – simply line the basket with
a silicone mat or baking parchment,
and cook them in batches. As for
brownies and blondies, just make
sure that your tin fits in your air fryer
and you're good to go!

BIRTHDAY CAKE SANDWICH COOKIES

200g (1¾ stick) unsalted butter, softened
50g (6 tbsp) icing (confectioners') sugar
200g (1½ cups) plain (all-purpose) flour
40g (6½ tbsp) cornflour (cornstarch)
1 tsp vanilla extract
1 tsp salt
100g (⅔ cup) white chocolate chips
3 tbsp sprinkles, plus extra to decorate

BUTTERCREAM FILLING:
100g (7 tbsp) unsalted butter, softened
200g (1½ cups) icing (confectioners') sugar, sifted
100g (scant ½ cup) cream cheese
1 tsp vanilla extract
1 tsp salt

1 Combine the butter and icing sugar in a mixing bowl, and beat with a wooden spoon for 2 minutes. Add the flour, cornflour, vanilla, and salt, and mix until a soft dough forms. Fold through the chocolate chips and sprinkles. Cover the dough and chill it for a minimum of 1 hour (and up to 1 day).

2 Prepare the buttercream filling while your dough is chilling. Place the softened butter in a large mixing bowl, and gradually add the sifted icing sugar, beating until fluffy. If you have an electric hand whisk, use this to speed up the process. Add the cream cheese, vanilla, and salt, then beat until combined. Set aside in the fridge.

3 Using a tablespoon measuring spoon, portion the dough into 24 scoops. Roll them into balls.

4 Preheat the air fryer to 160°C/325°F for 3 minutes. Line with a silicone mat.

5 Working in batches, if necessary, place the dough balls into the preheated lined air fryer basket, leaving a 5cm (2in) gap between them, as they will expand. Bake at 160°C/325°F for 12 minutes.

6 Leave the cookies to cool for 5 minutes before removing them from the air fryer basket with a spatula. Place on a wire rack to cool completely. Repeat the process until all the cookies are baked.

7 Take two cookies and sandwich them together with a spoonful of the buttercream filling, squeezing them together until the icing just escapes the sides. Roll the sides of each sandwiched cookie in sprinkles to decorate.

KEEP IT These will keep for 3 days in an airtight container in the fridge.

Prep + cook time
1 hour, plus chilling
Makes 12

DOUBLE-DECKER BROWNIE COOKIE SQUARES

COOKIE DOUGH:

80g (5½ tbsp) unsalted butter, softened

80g (6½ tbsp) soft light brown sugar

1 large (US extra large) egg, beaten

1 tsp vanilla extract

120g (scant 1 cup) plain (all-purpose) flour

½ tsp baking powder

½ tsp bicarbonate of soda (baking soda)

1 tsp sea salt

150g (1 cup) milk chocolate chips

BROWNIE BATTER:

100g (3½oz) dark (bittersweet) chocolate, roughly chopped

60g (½ stick) unsalted butter, cubed

80g (6½ tbsp) soft light brown sugar

1 large (US extra large) egg, beaten

½ tsp salt

20g (2 tbsp) plain (all-purpose) flour, sifted

150g (1 cup) white chocolate chips

1 For the cookie dough, beat the butter and sugar with a wooden spoon, then mix in the egg and vanilla. Sift in the flour and raising agents, then add the salt. Mix until smooth, then fold in the chocolate chips.

2 Scrape the dough into a 20cm (8in) lined brownie tin, pressing it in evenly. Place in the fridge while you make the brownie.

3 Melt the chocolate and butter in a small heatproof bowl set over a pan of simmering water, stirring. Remove from the heat and check the temperature of the mixture: it should be warm, not hot (if it's hot, let it cool for 5 minutes).

4 Whisk the sugar and egg together in a mixing bowl, then pour in the warm chocolate-butter mixture. Whisk until combined. Add the salt and flour, then fold through with a spatula. Fold in the chocolate chips.

5 Preheat the air fryer to 180°C/350°F for 3 minutes, and remove the tin from the fridge.

6 Bake in the air fryer for 10 minutes at 180°C/350°F. Tap on the surface to deflate the dough, then pour over the brownie batter, and smooth it with a spatula. Bake at 180°C/350°F for 14 minutes until it has a crisp crust, but a slight wobble. Cool in the tin on a wire rack, then put in the fridge to chill for 2–3 hours.

7 Once set, remove from the tin and cut into squares.

KEEP IT Keep for up to 5 days in an airtight container in the fridge.

**Prep + cook time
40 minutes, plus chilling
Makes 12**

OATMEAL, CANDIED ORANGE, & RAISIN COOKIES

100g (7 tbsp) unsalted butter, softened
150g (¾ cup) soft light brown sugar
1 large (US extra large) egg
100g (1 cup) rolled (old-fashioned) oats
200g (1½ cups) plain (all-purpose) flour
½ tsp bicarbonate of soda (baking soda)
½ tsp baking powder
1 tsp ground cinnamon
1 tsp salt
45g (⅓ cup) candied orange peel
75g (½ cup) raisins

1 Combine the softened butter and brown sugar in a large mixing bowl, and beat for 2 minutes until the mixture starts to become lighter in texture. Add the egg and oats, and mix until fully incorporated.

2 Sift in the flour, bicarbonate of soda, baking powder, cinnamon, and salt, and fold these into the batter until you have a soft cookie dough consistency. Finally, fold through the orange peel and raisins until evenly distributed.

3 Using scales, weigh out 50g (1¾oz) portions of dough. Roll each one between the palms of your hands and place in a lined airtight container (if you are double layering, separate the layers of cookie dough with a piece of greaseproof paper) and place in the fridge for at least 1 hour or overnight.

4 Preheat the air fryer to 170°C/340°F for 3 minutes and line the basket with a silicone mat or some baking parchment.

5 Put the chilled cookie dough portions into the lined preheated air fryer basket, leaving 5cm (2in) between each cookie. Bake for 15 minutes at 170°C/340°F.

6 Leave the cookies to cool for 5 minutes before removing them from the air fryer basket with a spatula. Place on a wire rack to cool completely.

KEEP IT Store for up to 5 days in an airtight container.

Prep + cook time
30 minutes, plus chilling
Makes 12

BROWN BUTTER & SALTED PECAN BLONDIES

200g (1¾ sticks) salted butter, cubed

300g (1½ cups) soft light brown sugar

2 eggs

2 tsp vanilla paste

250g (scant 2 cups) plain (all-purpose) flour

2 tsp cornflour (cornstarch)

100g (⅔ cup) white chocolate chips

75g (¾ cup) pecan halves, roughly chopped

2 tsp flaked sea salt

1 Place the butter in a small saucepan over a low heat. The butter will start to bubble and foam, then caramelize, and small brown flecks will start to appear. This will take 10–15 minutes, but keep checking and swirling the pan every couple of minutes, as it can suddenly change from golden to burnt. Once the liquid has turned a deep golden brown and smells toasted, remove from the heat and transfer the hot butter into a heatproof bowl to cool for 15 minutes.

2 Combine the cooled brown butter, sugar, eggs, and vanilla in a large mixing bowl, and whisk until the sugar has dissolved. Sift in the flour and cornflour, and mix until just combined, then add the chocolate chips and pecans. Give the batter a good mix until everything is evenly distributed.

3 Preheat the air fryer to 160°C/325°F for 3 minutes.

4 Pour the blondie batter into a 20cm (8in) lined brownie tin, and sprinkle with the flaked sea salt. Bake in the preheated air fryer at 160°C/325°F for 35 minutes until evenly golden with a firm crust, but a soft centre.

5 Leave to cool in the tin on a wire rack for 30 minutes, then place in the fridge to set overnight (or for at least 3 hours) before cutting into 9 large or 20 bite-sized pieces.

KEEP IT These will last for 5 days in an airtight container in the fridge, or can be frozen for up to 6 weeks.

Prep + cook time
1 hour, plus chilling
Makes 9 large or 20 bites

CHOCOLATE & HAZELNUT THUMBPRINT COOKIES

75g (¾ stick) unsalted butter, softened

40g (4½ tbsp) icing (confectioners') sugar

1 tsp vanilla paste

1 egg yolk

125g (scant 1 cup) plain (all-purpose) flour, plus extra for dusting

150g (generous 1 cup) hazelnuts, chopped

2 tsp flaked sea salt

150g (5¼oz) chocolate hazelnut spread

1 Beat the butter, icing sugar, vanilla, and egg yolk in a mixing bowl with a wooden spoon until combined. Mix in the flour until a soft dough forms.

2 Lay a 40cm/16in piece of clingfilm on the work surface. Place the dough in the centre of the clingfilm, and, using your hands, squeeze the dough to form a chunky sausage about 30cm (12in) long. Wrap it in the clingfilm, and place in the fridge for 20 minutes.

3 Place the chilled dough on a lightly floured surface. Slice the log into ten pieces, roughly 3cm (1¼in) thick. Using your palms, roll each piece into a ball.

4 Combine the chopped hazelnuts and flaked sea salt in a shallow bowl. One by one, place each dough ball into the mix, and roll it to coat in a layer of nuts.

5 Using a tablespoon measuring spoon, make an indent in the centre of each cookie.

6 Preheat the air fryer to 160°C/325°F for 3 minutes and line the basket with a silicone mat or some baking parchment.

7 Put the cookies in the lined preheated air fryer basket, leaving 5cm (2in) between each cookie. You may need to bake them in batches.

8 Bake at 160°C/325°F for 10–12 minutes until lightly golden brown. Continue to bake in batches until all the cookies are cooked.

9 Press down in the centre with the tablespoon measuring spoon again while they are still hot (as they will have puffed up slightly while cooking).

10 While still warm, spoon the chocolate hazelnut spread into the indents, and allow to cool.

KEEP IT These will keep for 5 days in an airtight container.

**Prep + cook time
40 minutes, plus chilling
Makes 10**

SESAME & DARK CHOCOLATE COOKIES

125g (9 tbsp) unsalted butter
30g (scant ⅓ cup) unsweetened
  cocoa powder
1 large (US extra large) egg, beaten
80g (6½ tbsp) soft light brown sugar
80g (6½ tbsp) golden caster
  (superfine) sugar
140g (1 cup plus 1 tbsp) plain
  (all-purpose) flour
½ tsp bicarbonate of soda
  (baking soda)
150g (1 cup) dark (bittersweet)
  chocolate chips
5 tbsp sesame seeds
1 tsp sea salt (optional)

1 Place the butter in a small saucepan on a low heat until melted, then stir in the cocoa until it becomes smooth and lump free. Take off the heat and set aside.

2 In a large mixing bowl, combine the beaten egg with the sugars, and whisk until the sugars have dissolved. Pour in the lukewarm melted butter and cocoa mix. Whisk again until combined.

3 Sift the flour and bicarbonate of soda into the batter, then stir until a soft dough forms. Once all the flour is absorbed, fold through the chocolate chips. Place the dough in the fridge for 30 minutes to firm up.

4 Once the dough has chilled, weigh out 60g (2oz) portions and roll into balls using the palms of your hands. Spread the sesame seeds out in a shallow bowl, then roll each dough ball in the seeds to coat.

5 Place the coated dough balls back into the fridge for 30 minutes (or up to overnight).

6 Preheat the air fryer to 180°C/350°F for 3 minutes and line the basket with a silicone mat or some baking parchment.

7 Put the chilled cookie dough portions in the lined preheated air fryer basket, leaving 5cm (2in) between each cookie, sprinkle with sea salt, if using, and bake at 180°C/350°F for 10 minutes.

8 Leave the cookies to cool in the air fryer basket until firm enough to remove with a spatula, then transfer to a wire rack to cool completely.

KEEP IT These will keep for up to 5 days in an airtight container.

Prep + cook time
30 minutes, plus chilling
Makes 10

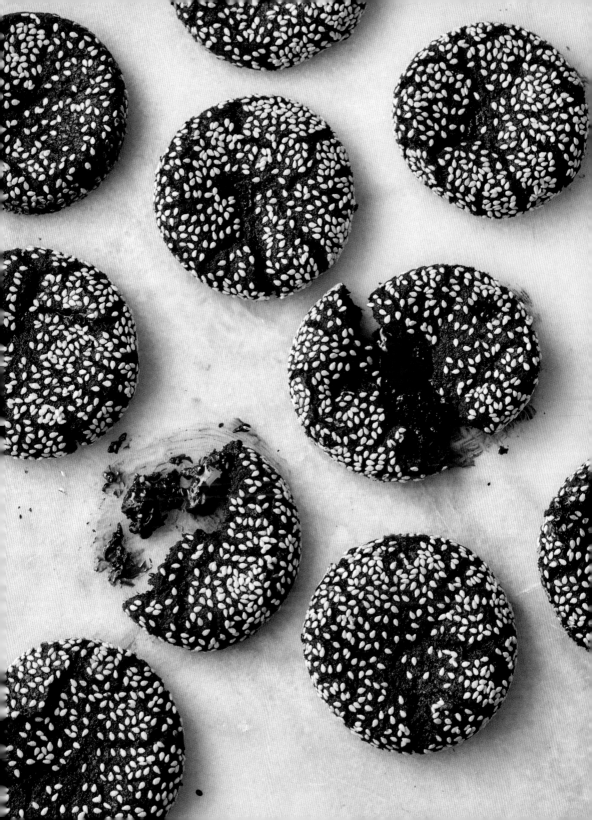

RASPBERRY CHEESECAKE BROWNIES

200g (7oz) dark (bittersweet) chocolate, roughly chopped
120g (1 stick) unsalted butter, cubed
120g (½ cup plus 4 tsp) light soft brown sugar
2 eggs
35g (¼ cup) plain (all-purpose) flour
1 tsp salt
100g (3½oz) raspberries

CHEESECAKE:
150g (⅔ cup) cream cheese
1 egg
1 tsp vanilla paste
2 tbsp caster (superfine) sugar
2 tsp cornflour (cornstarch)

1 Place the chocolate and butter in a heatproof bowl over a pan of simmering water. You want the bowl to rest 2.5cm (1in) above the water. Keep stirring until the chocolate has melted, then remove the bowl from the pan (taking care as the bowl will be very hot) and set aside to cool slightly.
2 Combine all the cheesecake ingredients in a medium mixing bowl and set aside.
3 In another mixing bowl, combine the light brown sugar and eggs, and whisk until the sugar starts to dissolve. Pour in the warm melted chocolate, whisk until fully combined, then fold through the flour and salt.
4 Pour the brownie mixture into a lined 20cm (8in) brownie tin, and spread it out evenly. Dollop the cheesecake mixture over the top. Using a skewer or knife, swirl the two batters together.

5 Sprinkle the raspberries all over, pushing some down so they are half-submerged by the batter.
6 Preheat the air fryer to 160°C/325°F for 3 minutes.
7 Place the brownie tin in the preheated air fryer, and bake for 25 minutes at 160°C/325°F until the cheesecake mix has started to brown and form a crust (the mix should be firm, but have a wobble if you gently shake the tin).
8 Leave to cool in the tin on a wire rack for 30 minutes before placing in the fridge to set overnight (or for at least 3 hours).
9 Cut into 9 large or 20 bite-sized pieces.

Prep + cook time
50 minutes, plus chilling
Makes 9 large or 20 bites

SALTED PRETZEL, FUDGE & PEANUT COOKIES

80g (5½ tbsp) unsalted butter, softened

100g (½ cup) dark soft brown sugar

3 tbsp crunchy peanut butter

1 large (US extra large) egg, beaten

150g (1 cup plus 2 tbsp) plain (all-purpose) flour

½ tsp baking powder

½ tsp bicarbonate of soda (baking soda)

1 tsp sea salt

100g (3½oz) fudge pieces

30g (1oz) salted pretzels, broken into pieces

30g (2 tbsp) roasted peanuts

1 In a large mixing bowl, combine the butter, sugar, and peanut butter. Beat with a wooden spoon until the mixture lightens. Add the egg and mix until combined. Sift in the flour and raising agents, then sprinkle in the sea salt. Mix until the flour is absorbed.

2 Fold through the fudge pieces, pretzel pieces, and roasted peanuts until evenly distributed.

3 Weigh the dough out into 50g (2oz) portions, then roll into balls using the palms of your hands. Place the rolled cookie dough onto a lined baking tray and put in the fridge for at least 30 minutes (or up to overnight) to firm up.

4 Preheat the air fryer to 180°C/350°F for 3 minutes and line the basket with a silicone mat or some baking parchment.

5 Carefully transfer each cookie to the lined air fryer basket, leaving 5cm (2in) between them. Bake for 10–12 minutes at 180°C/ 350°F until they're lightly golden brown.

6 Leave the cookies to cool in the air fryer basket until firm enough to remove with a spatula, then transfer to a wire rack to cool completely.

KEEP IT Store for up to 5 days in an airtight container.

Prep + cook time 30 minutes, plus chilling Makes 10

ICED VANILLA BISCUITS

75g (¾ stick) unsalted butter, softened
30g (2½ tbsp) caster (superfine) sugar
½ tsp salt
1 tsp vanilla paste
100g (¾ cup) plain (all-purpose) flour

ICING:
200g (1½ cups) royal icing sugar
2–5 drops of chosen food colouring

TIP If you can't find royal icing sugar, make your own by combining 400g (3 cups) sifted icing (confectioners') sugar, 2 tbsp dried egg white, and the juice of ½ lemon, and beating into a thick, smooth icing that will drizzle but hold its form.

1 Beat the butter, caster sugar, salt, and vanilla in a mixing bowl with a wooden spoon until light and fluffy. Sift in the flour and stir until a soft dough forms.
2 Weigh the dough into 20g (¾oz) portions, then roll into balls with the palms of your hands. Place onto a lined baking tray with a 5cm (2in) gap between them. Using a flat-bottomed glass, press each ball to flatten it. Chill in the fridge for 30 minutes.
3 Preheat the air fryer to 180°C/350°F for 3 minutes and line the basket with a silicone mat or some baking parchment.
4 Transfer each biscuit to the lined air fryer basket. Bake for 8–12 minutes at 180°C/350°F until they're lightly golden brown.
5 Leave in the basket for a few minutes, then transfer to a wire rack to cool.
6 For the icing, sift the royal icing sugar into a large mixing bowl, then add 2 tablespoons water.

7 Bring together with a spatula until you have a smooth icing, then whisk with a hand-held electric whisk for 5 minutes until the mix doubles in size and leaves stiff peaks when you lift the beaters out of the bowl. At this point you can colour the icing: either divide amongst smaller bowls to make multiple colours, or use just one (add the colouring drop by drop until you have your desired shade).
8 Put a piping (pastry) bag fitted with a nozzle in a tall glass, rolling the excess over the sides. Spoon in the icing. Decorate the biscuits in your chosen design, then leave to set for at least 1 hour (or up to overnight).

KEEP IT These will keep for 5–7 days in an airtight container.

Prep + cook time
30 minutes, plus chilling
Makes 10

CORNFLAKE COOKIES

100g (7 tbsp) unsalted butter, softened
100g (½ cup) soft light brown sugar
1 large (US extra large) egg, beaten
1 tsp vanilla extract
150g (1 cup plus 2 tbsp) plain (all-purpose) flour
½ tsp baking powder
½ tsp bicarbonate of soda (baking soda)
1 tsp salt
50g (2 cups) cornflakes
20g (5 tbsp) freeze-dried strawberries
100g (⅔ cup) white chocolate chips

1 Combine the butter and sugar in a medium mixing bowl. Beat with a wooden spoon until combined, then pour in the beaten egg and vanilla. Mix again until they start to come together (don't worry if the mixture looks split; as soon as you add the dry ingredients a smooth dough will form).

2 Sift the flour and raising agents into the bowl, then sprinkle in the salt. Mix until all the flour is absorbed and you have a smooth cookie dough. Fold through the cornflakes, strawberries, and chocolate chips until they are evenly distributed.

3 Weigh the dough out into 50g (2oz) portions, then roll into balls using the palms of your hands. If the dough is very soft and sticky, place it in the fridge for 30 minutes to firm up before rolling into balls.

4 Place the rolled cookies on a lined baking tray and put in the fridge for at least 30 minutes (or up to overnight) before baking.

5 Preheat the air fryer to 180°C/350°F for 3 minutes and line the basket with a silicone mat or some baking parchment.

6 Put the cookies in the lined air fryer basket, leaving 5cm (2in) between each cookie. Bake for 10 minutes at 180°C/350°F, or until light golden brown.

7 Leave to cool in the air fryer basket until firm enough to remove with a spatula, then transfer to a wire rack to cool completely.

KEEP IT These cookies will keep for up to 5 days in an airtight container.

Prep + cook time
30 minutes, plus chilling
Makes 12

BROWNIE MUD PIE

300g (10½oz) dark (bittersweet) chocolate, roughly chopped
180g (1½ sticks) butter, cubed
180g (1 cup minus 1½ tbsp) light soft brown sugar
3 eggs, beaten
1 tsp sea salt
60g (scant ½ cup) plain (all-purpose) flour
100g (3½oz) milk chocolate, chopped
100g (3½oz) dark (bittersweet) chocolate, chopped

BASE:
200g (7oz) ginger nuts (ginger snaps), crushed
75g (¾ stick) unsalted butter, melted
1 tsp flaked sea salt

1 Start by making the base. Crush the ginger nuts into a fine sandy crumb in a blender or by bashing with a rolling pin. Mix with the melted butter and sea salt until coated.
2 Spoon the mixture into a greased 20–23cm (8–9in) loose-bottomed round tin. Use the back of a spoon to press the crumbs into the base and 1cm (½in) up the sides. Place in the fridge to chill while you make the brownie batter.
3 Melt the chocolate and butter in a small heatproof bowl set over a pan of simmering water, stirring. Remove from the heat and check the temperature of the mixture: it should be warm, not hot (if it's hot, let it cool for 5 minutes).
4 Whisk the sugar and eggs in a mixing bowl, then pour in the warm chocolate butter mix. Whisk until fully combined (the mixture should start to thicken as this happens).

5 Add the salt to the batter and sift in the flour, then fold these through with a spatula until the flour is all absorbed. Add the chopped chocolate and fold in until evenly distributed.
6 Preheat the air fryer to 160°C/325°F for 3 minutes.
7 Remove the tin from the fridge and pour in the brownie batter. Place in the air fryer basket and bake for 30 minutes at 160°C/325°F until firm, but with a slight wobble.
8 Place on a wire rack and leave to cool completely in the tin, then place in the fridge for at least 1 hour (and up to overnight).
9 Once chilled, release from the tin and slice into wedges.

KEEP IT This pie will keep for up to 5 days in an airtight container.

**Prep + cook time
1 hour, plus chilling
Serves 10**

CAKES

From indulgent chocolate stout cake to sprinkle-topped baked doughnuts, your air fryer will bake all manner of cakes to perfection. You can buy silicone moulds that are designed for air fryers, or use small loaf tins, cakes tins, or pudding tins – and simply bake in batches if needed.

FIERY GINGER CAKE

2 large (US extra large) eggs
120ml (½ cup) vegetable oil
50g (1¾oz) black treacle
150g (¾ cup) dark muscovado sugar
150g (1 cup plus 2 tbsp) self-raising (self-rising) flour
2 tsp ground ginger
1 tsp ground cinnamon
1 tsp allspice
1 tsp ground black pepper
1 tsp salt
40g (1½oz) candied ginger in syrup, finely chopped

SYRUP:
juice of 1 orange
juice of 1 lime
1 piece of stem ginger, finely diced
50g (¼ cup) dark soft brown sugar

TIP This can be served as is, or toasted and spread with butter.

1 Combine the eggs, oil, treacle, and sugar in a medium mixing bowl, and whisk until fully combined. Sift in the dry ingredients, continuing to whisk until just combined, then fold in the finely chopped ginger.

2 Preheat the air fryer to 160°C/325°F for 3 minutes.

3 Pour the cake batter into a greased and lined 450g (1lb) loaf tin, and cook in the preheated air fryer for 40 minutes at 160°C/325°F until an inserted skewer comes out clean (if the skewer has wet cake batter on it, continue to bake the sponge at 5-minute intervals until the skewer is clean).

4 Remove the tin from the air fryer and leave to cool on a wire rack while you make the syrup.

5 Place all the syrup ingredients in small pan over a medium heat, bring to a gentle simmer, and cook for 5 minutes.

6 Turn out the cooled loaf and place on a rimmed plate or in a clean baking tray. Spoon over the hot syrup, then leave to cool fully before removing from the tray.

KEEP IT Store for up to 5 days in an airtight container.

Prep + cook time
1 hour
Serves 8–10

CHOCOLATE STOUT CAKE WITH CREAM CHEESE FROSTING

225g (2 sticks) unsalted butter
60g (scant ⅔ cup) unsweetened
  cocoa powder, plus extra
  to decorate
225ml (scant 1 cup) stout
200g (1 cup) caster (superfine) sugar
180g (1 cup minus 1½ tbsp) light soft
  brown sugar
2 large (US extra large) eggs, beaten
150g (¾ cup) plain yogurt
1 tsp vanilla extract
scant 2 cups (250g) plain
  (all-purpose) flour
1 tsp bicarbonate of soda
  (baking soda)
1 tsp baking powder

ICING:
150g (1¼ sticks) unsalted butter,
  softened
300g (2 cups plus 2 tbsp) icing
  (confectioners') sugar
1 tsp fine salt
1 tsp vanilla extract
300g (1⅓ cups) full-fat cream cheese

1 Place the butter in a medium saucepan and melt over a low heat. Whisk in the cocoa and stout until you have a lump-free liquid, then remove from the heat. Set aside to cool until the mixture is lukewarm.
2 Whisk together the sugars, eggs, yogurt, and vanilla in a large mixing bowl, then pour in the lukewarm butter-cocoa mixture. Whisk again until combined.
3 Sift the flour and raising agents into the batter and whisk until all the flour is absorbed.
4 Preheat the air fryer to 160°C/325°F for 3 minutes.
5 Pour the batter into a greased and lined 20–23cm (8–9in) loose-bottomed cake tin. Bake at 160°C/325°F for 1 hour.
6 Leave to cool in the tin on a wire rack for 30 minutes, then turn out and leave to cool completely.

7 While the cake is cooling, prepare the icing. Beat the softened butter until light, then gradually sift in the icing sugar, beating until it is fluffy and airy. Stir through the salt and vanilla extract, then finally fold through the cream cheese. Beat until this is fully combined and the icing is smooth. Place the icing in the fridge to firm up while the cake continues to cool.
8 Once the cake is cold, place it on a platter or plate, then dollop on the icing. Smooth it with a spoon, then dust the cake with cocoa to decorate.

KEEP IT This cake will keep for 3 days in an airtight container in the fridge.

**Prep + cook time
2 hours
Serves 8–12**

TOASTED S'MORES CAKE

250g (1¼ cups) caster (superfine)
    sugar
2 large (US extra large) eggs
90ml (⅓ cup) vegetable oil
180g (generous ¾ cup) plain yogurt
1½ tsp vanilla extract
250g (scant 2 cups) plain
    (all-purpose) flour
1 tsp baking powder
1 tsp bicarbonate of soda
    (baking soda)
160ml (⅔ cup) boiling water
150g (5¼oz) store-bought cookies,
    crushed, plus extra to decorate
to decorate: marshmallows, edible
    gold leaf, gold chocolate balls,
    and indoor sparklers (optional)

CHOCOLATE GANACHE:
300ml (1¼ cups) double (heavy)
    cream
4 tbsp golden syrup
300g (10½oz) dark (bittersweet)
    chocolate, finely chopped

1 Place the sugar, eggs, oil, yogurt, and vanilla extract into a large mixing bowl. Whisk until combined, then sift in the dry ingredients. Whisk until all the flour is incorporated, then add the boiling water and whisk until you have a runny cake batter. (It may seem odd to pour boiling water into cake mix, but this results in a delicious moist but chewy sponge.)
2 Preheat the air fryer to 180°C/350°F for 3 minutes.
3 Pour the cake batter into a greased and lined 20cm (8in) round cake tin, then crumble over the crushed cookies. Place the tin in the preheated air fryer and bake for 35 minutes at 180°C/350°F until the crust is a deep golden colour and an inserted skewer comes out clean.
4 Leave to cool on a wire rack for 15 minutes, then turn the cake out of the tin and let cool completely.

5 While the cake is cooling, you can make the chocolate ganache. Gently heat the double cream in a small saucepan with the golden syrup. Place the chopped chocolate in a medium heatproof bowl. When the cream mixture is steaming hot, pour it over the chocolate. Leave it to sit for 30 seconds, then stir until all the chocolate has melted.
6 Once the sponge has cooled, top with chocolate ganache and decorate with extra crumbled cookies, some marshmallows, edible gold leaf, gold chocolate balls, and indoor sparklers, if you like.

KEEP IT This cake will keep for up to 3 days stored in an airtight container.

**Prep + cook time
1 hour
Serves 8–12**

85

ORANGE, FENNEL & POLENTA CAKE
(GLUTEN-FREE)

1 orange
100g (3½oz) olive oil
100g (½ cup) caster (superfine) sugar
1 tsp ground fennel seeds
2 large (US extra large) eggs, beaten
50g (¼ cup) Greek or plain yogurt
150g (1 cup) coarse polenta (cornmeal)
80g (¾ cup) ground almonds

1 Start by preparing the orange purée. Pierce the whole orange multiple times with a fork, then place in a small saucepan of water. Bring to the boil and simmer gently for 15 minutes until the orange becomes tender. Remove from the water, place in a blender, and blend to a coarse pulp. Alternatively, if you do not have blender, leave the orange to cool, then chop using a large knife into a pulp.
2 In a large mixing bowl, combine all the remaining ingredients. Beat with a wooden spoon until you have a smooth batter. Fold through the orange pulp.
3 Preheat the air fryer to 180°C/350°F for 3 minutes.

4 Grease 6–8 metal pudding tins and dust with polenta. Fill each tin three-quarters full with cake mixture, then bake in the air fryer for 15 minutes at 180°C/350°F.
5 Turn out onto a wire rack and leave to cool for 15 minutes, then either serve warm or leave to cool completely.

KEEP IT Will keep for up to 5 days in an airtight container.

SERVE IT Serve warm with Greek yogurt and honey.

**Prep + cook time
1 hour
Makes 6–8**

COCONUT & RASPBERRY LAMINGTONS

120g (1 stick) unsalted butter, softened
½ cup plus 4 tsp (120g) caster (superfine) sugar
2 large (US extra large) eggs
1 tsp vanilla paste
1 tsp salt
scant 1 cup (120g) self-raising (self-rising) flour
2 tbsp raspberry jam

COATING:
100g (3½oz) dark (bittersweet) chocolate, finely chopped
2 tbsp (30g) unsalted butter
⅔ cup (50g) desiccated (dried unsweetened) coconut

1 Combine the softened butter, sugar, eggs, vanilla, and salt in a medium bowl. Beat until combined, then sift in the flour. Mix until you have smooth batter.

2 Preheat the air fryer to 160°C/325°F for 3 minutes.

3 Divide the cake batter amongst eight square silicone brownie moulds. Bake in the preheated air fryer for 12 minutes at 160°C/325°F (you may need to do this in batches) until light golden brown and the sponge bounces back when pressed.

4 Remove from the air fryer and leave to cool on a wire rack in the silicone moulds for 5 minutes. While still warm, pop the sponges out of the moulds, then leave to cool completely before icing.

5 Meanwhile, for the coating, melt the chopped chocolate and butter in a heatproof bowl over a pan of simmering water. Set aside.

6 Take one sponge cake and place ½ tbsp jam on top, spreading it out to the edges using the back of the spoon. Place a second sponge on top. Place the layered cakes back onto the wire rack.

7 Using a pastry brush, cover each cake with the chocolate coating.

8 Place the desiccated coconut on a plate, then roll each lamington in coconut until each side is coated.

KEEP IT These will keep for 3 days in an airtight container.

**Prep + cook time
1 hour
Makes 4**

89

NEAPOLITAN CAKE

300g (1½ cups) plain yogurt
180ml (¾ cup) vegetable oil
3 large (US extra large) eggs
225g (1 cup plus 2 tbsp) caster
    (superfine) sugar
1 tsp vanilla extract
1 tsp salt
300g (2¼ cups) self-raising
    (self-rising) flour, plus 2 tbsp
    for the strawberry sponge
1 tsp baking powder
2 tbsp unsweetened cocoa powder
½ tsp pink food colouring
6 strawberries, crushed
6 strawberries, sliced
To decorate: chocolate sprinkles,
    wafers, and strawberries

ICING:
200g (1¾ sticks) unsalted butter,
    softened
400g (scant 3 cups) icing
    (confectioners') sugar
200g (scant 1 cup) cream cheese
1 tsp vanilla extract
1 tsp salt
½ tsp pink food colouring

1 Combine the yogurt, oil, eggs, sugar, vanilla, and salt in a bowl. Sift in the flour and baking powder. Whisk until smooth.
2 Divide the batter equally amongst three bowls. Set one aside as it is. Add the cocoa to the second bowl. To the final bowl, add the colouring, crushed strawberries, and extra 2 tablespoons flour.
3 Preheat the air fryer to 160°C/325°F for 3 minutes.
4 Dollop spoonfuls of each cake batter into two greased and lined 20cm (8in) round tins. Using a skewer, swirl the three batters together.
5 Bake each cake in the preheated air fryer for 25 minutes at 160°C/ 325°F until an inserted skewer comes out clean.
6 For the icing, beat the butter in a mixing bowl, gradually adding the icing sugar, until fluffy. Beat in the cream cheese, vanilla, and salt. Set aside.

7 Remove one-third of the icing and set aside. Add the pink food colouring to the rest and mix well.
8 Once the sponges are baked, place on a wire rack to cool for 15 minutes in their tins, then turn out and leave to cool completely.
9 Place each buttercream in a piping (pastry) bag fitted with a star nozzle.
10 Place a layer of sponge onto a cake plate, pipe with pink buttercream, then add the sliced strawberries on top. Place the second cake on top, bottom-side down. Pipe the rest of the pink icing in swirls on the top. Pipe swirls of white icing in the gaps, then decorate with chocolate sprinkles, wafers, and strawberries.

KEEP IT Store in an airtight container in the fridge for 3 days.

**Cook + prep time
2 hours
Serves 8–12**

UPSIDE-DOWN MARMALADE CAKE

200g (⅔ cup) thick-cut marmalade
180g (1½ sticks) unsalted butter, softened
180g (1 cup minus 1½ tbsp) golden caster (superfine) sugar
grated zest of 1 orange
3 large (US extra large) eggs, beaten
75ml (5 tbsp) kefir
1 tsp sea salt
180g (1⅓ cups) self-raising (self-rising) flour

1 Spoon the marmalade into the base of a greased 20cm (8in) loose-bottomed round tin, and spread it out to create an even layer using the back of the spoon. Set aside while you make the cake sponge.
2 In a medium mixing bowl, combine the butter, sugar, and orange zest, beating with a wooden spoon for 5 minutes until light and fluffy.
3 Pour the beaten eggs and kefir into the bowl, beat to combine, then sprinkle in the salt and sift in the flour. Continue mixing until the batter is a smooth consistency and all the flour is absorbed.
4 Preheat the air fryer to 180°C/350°F for 3 minutes.

5 Transfer the cake batter to the tin, then bake in the air fryer for 35–40 minutes at 180°C/350°F. The crust should be a deep golden brown and the sponge should be firm to touch.
6 Transfer to a wire rack to cool for 20–30 minutes until cool enough to handle, but still warm, then flip it out onto a plate. (The cake needs to be turned out while still warm so that the marmalade doesn't set to the tin.)

KEEP IT Keep for up to 5 days in an airtight container.

Prep + cook time
1 hour
Serves 8

SPICED BROWN SUGAR, LIME & PINEAPPLE LOAF

227g (8oz) can pineapple chunks in juice
grated zest and juice of 1 lime
½ tsp chilli flakes
140g (¾ cup) light soft brown sugar
120g (1 stick) salted butter, softened
grated zest and juice of 1 orange
2 large (US extra large) eggs
120g (scant 1 cup) self-raising (self-rising) flour
50g (¼ cup) caster (superfine) sugar

TIP Eat while still warm with a scoop of mango sorbet and grating of lime zest, or leave to cool and eat simply by the slice with a coffee.

1 Drain the can of pineapple over a sieve and reserve the juice for the syrup. Place the pineapple chunks, lime zest, chilli flakes, and 20g (2 tbsp) brown sugar in a medium bowl, and mix until combined and the sugar has dissolved. Pour the pineapple chunks into a greased 450g (1lb) loaf tin and set aside.

2 Combine the softened butter, orange zest, and remaining brown sugar in a medium mixing bowl, and beat for 5 minutes until the mixture becomes fluffier in texture. Add the eggs, and mix until just combined. Sift in the flour and mix until you have a smooth batter.

3 Preheat the air fryer to 160°C/325°F for 3 minutes.

4 Give the tin a little jiggle to distribute the pineapple chunks along the base, then spoon in the batter, and spread it out evenly.

5 Bake in the preheated air fryer for 40 minutes at 160°C/325°F.

6 Meanwhile, make the syrup. Combine the reserved pineapple juice, the orange juice, lime juice, and caster sugar in a small saucepan over a high heat for 5 minutes. Let cool.

7 The cake is ready when it has a deep golden brown crust and an inserted skewer comes out clean. Leave to cool on a wire rack for 10 minutes.

8 Use a skewer or fork to pierce the sponge all over. Pour half the syrup onto the warm cake and leave to absorb for 10 minutes, then turn the cake out onto a plate and pour over the remaining syrup.

KEEP IT This cake will keep in an airtight container for up to 3 days.

**Prep + cook time
1 hour
Serves 8**

BAKED DOUGHUTS WITH VANILLA GLAZE

100g (3½oz) vegetable oil
2 large (US extra large) eggs
100g (½ cup) caster (superfine)
    sugar
1 tsp vanilla extract
100g (¾ cup) self-raising
    (self-rising) flour

ICING:
100g (¾ cup) icing (confectioners')
    sugar
½ tsp vanilla extract
½ tsp ground cinnamon

DECORATION:
3 tbsp sprinkles

1 In a large mixing bowl, whisk the oil, eggs, sugar, and vanilla together until combined. Sift in the flour and whisk again until you have a smooth batter.
2 Preheat the air fryer to 180°C/350°F for 3 minutes.
3 Fill 12 silicone doughnut moulds three-quarters full with batter. Transfer to the air fryer basket and bake for 8 minutes at 180°C/350°F until lightly golden and firm to touch.
4 Remove the baked doughnuts from the moulds and leave to cool on a wire rack.
5 Meanwhile, make the icing. Sift the icing sugar into a bowl, then combine with the vanilla, cinnamon, and 1 tablespoon water until smooth.

6 One by one, dunk the top of each cooled doughnut into the icing, then place back onto the wire rack, and scatter with sprinkles. Leave for 30 minutes for the icing to set, then serve.

KEEP IT The doughnuts will keep for up to 5 days in an airtight container.

**Prep + cook time
30 minutes
Makes 12**

CHERRY & ALMOND CAKE

100g (7 tbsp) unsalted butter, softened
100g (½ cup) caster (superfine) sugar
grated zest of 1 lemon
2 large (US extra large) eggs
80g (¾ cup) ground almonds
80g (scant ⅔ cup) self-raising (self-rising) flour
½ tsp baking powder
½ tsp salt
150g (5¼oz) cherries, pitted and halved
1 tbsp cornflour (cornstarch)
3 tbsp cherry jam
8 cherries, to decorate

ICING:
150g (1 cup) icing (confectioners') sugar
25g (¾oz) cherry jam
juice of ½ lemon

1 Combine the softened butter, sugar, and lemon zest in a mixing bowl, and beat for 5 minutes until fluffy. Add the eggs and ground almonds, and mix until combined. Sift in the flour, baking powder, and salt, and fold in until just incorporated.
2 In a small bowl, combine the pitted cherries with the cornflour, and stir until coated. Fold the coated cherries into the batter.
3 Preheat the air fryer to 180°C/350°F for 3 minutes.
4 Pour one-quarter of the cake batter into a greased and floured 450g (1lb) pudding tin, then top with 1 tablespoon cherry jam, and spread the jam with the back of the spoon. Repeat with two more layers of batter and jam, and finish with a layer of batter. Smooth the surface.
5 Bake in the preheated air fryer for 10 minutes at 180°C/350°F.

6 Turn the temperature down to 160°C/325°F and cook for 45 minutes until an inserted skewer comes out clean. Do not to open the air fryer until the cake has been cooking for at least 35 minutes, otherwise it may collapse.
7 Leave to cool in the tin for 30 minutes.
8 Meanwhile, make the icing. Sift the icing sugar into a bowl, then mix in the cherry jam and lemon juice. The icing should have a thick consistency, and run slowly when you lift up the spoon; add more icing sugar if needed to thicken.
9 Once the cake has cooled fully, turn it out and cover the top in icing, allowing it to drip down the sides. Top with cherries.

KEEP IT This will keep for up to 3 days in an airtight container.

**Cook + prep time
1 hour 30 minutes
Serves 6–8**

PASTRY

Whether you're making your own shortcrust or using sheets of ready-rolled puff pastry, you will find it can be transformed into crispy savoury rolls or sweet pies in no time. Filo pastry also features in this chapter, as the heat of the air fryer crisps it to fabulously flaky perfection.

FENNEL & CHILLI SAUSAGE ROLLS

400g (14oz) sausage meat
1 tsp fennel seeds, plus extra
   to garnish
1 tsp chilli flakes
½ tsp garlic powder
1 tsp salt
320g (11oz) sheet of puff pastry
100g (3½oz) tomato and chilli
   chutney
1 egg, beaten
flaked sea salt, to garnish
to serve: chutney (optional)

1 Place the sausage meat in a mixing bowl, add the fennel seeds, chilli flakes, garlic powder, and salt, and give it a good few twists of black pepper. Use your hands to mix. Set aside.
2 Unroll the puff pastry, keeping it on the sheet of paper. Cut it lengthways in half. Separate the pieces slightly so you have some room to work.
3 Using a small spoon, spread half the chutney down the centre of each piece of pastry, in a strip about 2.5cm (1in) wide.
4 Take half the sausage meat and start to form a sausage on the chutney. Use your hands to mould it gently; it should be about 4cm (1½in) thick and the whole length of the pastry.
5 Using a pastry brush, brush beaten egg along the bottom edge of pastry. Take the top edge of the pastry and gently lift it over the sausage meat to meet the egg-washed edge.

6 Use your hands to mould the pastry around the meat, ensuring there are no gaps. Crimp along the whole length with a fork and trim off uneven edges.
7 Brush with egg, then garnish with flaked sea salt and fennel seeds. Cut each roll into three pieces.
8 Place the sausage rolls on a lined baking tray. Chill in the fridge for 15 minutes (or up to overnight).
9 Preheat the air fryer to 180°C/350°F for 3 minutes.
10 Place directly into the preheated air fryer basket and bake at 180°C/350°F for 16 minutes, or until deep golden. Cool for 10 minutes before serving.

KEEP IT Keep for up to 3 days in an airtight container in the fridge. Warm using the re-heat setting on your air fryer.

**Prep + cook time
45 minutes, plus chilling
Makes 6**

CURRIED POTATO & MANGO CHUTNEY PASTIES

1 small onion, finely chopped
1 garlic clove, grated
2.5cm (1in) piece of ginger, finely chopped
½ tsp mustard seeds
1 tsp cumin seeds
½ tsp nigella seeds
1 tsp curry powder
1 tsp sea salt
2 tbsp vegetable oil
350g (12oz) potato, peeled and cubed
5 tbsp mango chutney
2 tbsp chopped coriander (cilantro)
1 egg, beaten
1 tsp nigella seeds
to serve: raita or extra mango chutney

PASTRY:
300g (2¼ cups) plain (all-purpose) flour, plus extra for dusting
150g (1¼ sticks) unsalted butter, cold
1 tsp sea salt
3 tbsp cold water

1 Preheat the air fryer to 180°C/350°F for 3 minutes.
2 Combine the onion, garlic, ginger, spices, salt, and oil in a heatproof dish. Bake for 10 minutes at 180°C/350°F, then add the cubed potato, and bake for another 10 minutes. Stir and bake for a further 10 minutes, then set aside to cool.
3 For the pastry, place the flour in a mixing bowl. Using the largest side on a box grater, grate the cold butter into the bowl. Using your fingers, rub the butter into the flour until it's a sandy consistency. Add the salt and cold water, and knead the pastry until it comes together into a smooth ball. Wrap the pastry in clingfilm, then flatten into a disc. Chill in the fridge for 30 minutes.
4 Place the chilled pastry on a lightly floured work surface and roll out to 1cm (½in) thick.

5 Cut out an 18cm (7in) pastry circle. Re-roll the offcuts to cut another circle the same size.
6 Combine the potato filling, mango chutney, and coriander. Divide between the pastry circles. Pile the filling on the right-hand side of each circle, leaving a 2.5cm (1in) border.
7 Brush the border with beaten egg. Lift the left side of the pastry over the filling. Using a thumb and two fingers, crimp the pastry edge. Brush with egg, then sprinkle with the nigella seeds. Cut a 1cm (½in) hole in the centre for steam to escape.
8 Place directly into the air fryer basket and bake for 25 minutes at 180°C/350°F, or until deep golden brown. Cool for 10 minutes before serving with raita or extra mango chutney.

**Prep + cook time
1 hour, plus chilling
Makes 2**

THAI-STYLE SWEET POTATO ROLLS

2 sweet potatoes, peeled and cubed
1 small red onion, finely chopped
2.5cm (1in) piece of ginger, finely chopped
1 stick lemongrass, finely chopped
1 tsp flaked sea salt
2 tsp vegetable oil
grated zest and juice of 1 lime
2 tbsp coriander (cilantro), chopped
3 tbsp crunchy peanut butter
160ml (⅔ cup) canned creamed coconut
320g (11oz) sheet of puff pastry
1 egg, beaten
2 tbsp crushed peanuts
to serve: sweet chilli sauce

1 Preheat the air fryer to 180°C/350°F for 3 minutes.
2 Combine the sweet potatoes, onion, ginger, lemongrass, salt, and oil in a mixing bowl. Put into a heatproof dish and roast for 15 minutes at 180°C/350°F, stirring halfway through, until the sweet potato is soft when pierced with a knife.
3 Pour the filling back into the mixing bowl and mix in the lime zest and juice, coriander, peanut butter, and coconut cream. Set aside to cool completely.
4 Unroll the sheet of puff pastry, keeping it on the sheet of paper. Cut it in half lengthways, then divide the filling between the pieces of pastry, placing it down the centre of each piece to form a long sausage.
5 Brush egg along the bottom edge of the pastry. Take the top edge of the pastry and gently lift it over the sausage meat to meet the egg-washed edge.

6 Use your hands to mould the pastry around the filling, ensuring there are no gaps. Crimp along the whole length with a fork and trim off uneven edges. Slide the paper onto a baking tray and chill in the fridge for 15 minutes.
7 Trim off the ends of the rolls and discard. Brush the rolls with beaten egg and sprinkle with the crushed peanuts. Cut each roll into six pieces.
8 Preheat the air fryer to 180°C/350°F for 3 minutes.
9 Bake for 12–15 minutes at 180°C/350°F, or until deep golden brown and crisp. Leave to cool for 10 minutes before serving warm with sweet chilli sauce for dipping.

KEEP IT They will keep for up to 3 days in the fridge in an airtight container.

**Prep + cook time
1 hour, plus chilling
Makes 12**

FETA & SPINACH PIE

600g (1lb 5oz) baby spinach, wilted
1 leek, thinly sliced
1 tbsp olive oil
grated zest of 1 lemon
1 garlic clove, crushed
4 tbsp finely chopped parsley
4 tbsp finely chopped dill
4 tbsp finely chopped mint
2 large (US extra large) eggs, beaten
200g (7oz) feta, crumbled
100g (7 tbsp) unsalted butter, melted
320g (11oz) pack of filo pastry,
   defrosted if frozen
2 tsp sesame seeds
2 tsp nigella seeds
flaked sea salt, for sprinkling

TIP You can also use frozen spinach. Defrost it and squeeze out the excess water before using.

1 Cover the spinach in boiling water for 1 minute, then drain and cool. Once cool, squeeze the spinach tightly, draining out excess water. Set aside in a bowl.
2 Preheat the air fryer to 180°C/350°F for 3 minutes.
3 Put the leek into a heatproof dish with the oil and a sprinkle of salt. Place in the air fryer and cook at 180°C/350°F for 10 minutes, stirring halfway through. Combine with the spinach.
4 Add the lemon zest, garlic, and herbs, and season with black pepper. Add the eggs and combine. Fold in the feta, leaving nice chunks of cheese in the filling. Set aside.
5 Brush melted butter inside a deep 20cm (8in) loose-bottomed tin. Layer half the filo pastry in the tin, brushing each layer generously with butter, and letting the edges overhang the sides of the tin.

6 Add the spinach and feta mixture, then fold in the overhanging pastry edges to cover the filling.
7 Brush a sheet of the remaining pastry with butter, scrunch it up, and place on top of the pie. Repeat with the remaining pastry until the pie is covered. Sprinkle with the seeds and some flaked sea salt.
8 Preheat the air fryer to 180°C/350°F for 3 minutes.
9 Place the pie in the preheated air fryer basket and cook at 180°C/350°F for 20 minutes. Reduce the heat to 160°C/325°F and bake for 20 minutes more.
10 Carefully remove the side of the tin, then place the pie back in the air fryer for 20 minutes to crisp up the sides. Leave to cool for 10 minutes before cutting.

Prep + cook time
1 hour 30 minutes
Serves 6–8

SAUSAGE RAGU PIE

2 banana shallots, thinly sliced
1 stick of celery, thinly sliced
1 carrot, finely chopped
2 tbsp olive oil
400g (14oz) sausage meat
1 garlic clove, crushed
400g (14oz) can chopped plum
  tomatoes
50ml (3½ tbsp) red wine
100g (3½oz) Romano red peppers,
  roughly chopped
1 bay leaf
3 sprigs of rosemary
1 egg, beaten
flaked sea salt

SHORTCRUST PASTRY:
200g (1½ cups) plain (all-purpose)
  flour, plus extra for dusting
100g (7 tbsp) salted butter, cold
4 tbsp cold water

1 For the pastry, place the flour in a bowl. Using a box grater, grate in the butter. Rub the flour and butter together until you have a chunky crumb. Add the cold water and mix with your hands until the dough forms a shaggy ball.

2 Knead the dough gently on a lightly floured surface for 30 seconds until all the flour is absorbed, but you can still see flecks of butter. Form it into a 2.5cm (1in) thick disc, wrap in clingfilm, and chill it while you make the filling.

3 Preheat the air fryer to 190°C/375°F for 3 minutes.

4 Place the shallots, celery, and carrot in a heatproof dish with the olive oil and a sprinkle of salt. Roast in the air fryer at 190°C/375°F for 10 minutes. Stir, then add the sausage meat and roast for 10 minutes. Use a spoon to break up the meat, then add the garlic, canned tomatoes, and red wine.

5 Use 100ml (⅓ cup) water to rinse the tomato can and add this, along with the Romano peppers. Stir, then submerge the bay leaf and rosemary. Roast for 40 minutes at 190°C/375°F, stirring halfway through.

6 Spoon the ragu into a 22cm (9in) metal pie tin. Let cool for 30 minutes.

7 Roll out the pastry to a 25cm (10in) disc. Brush the edges of the dish with egg, then add the pastry lid. Press the edges down to seal it to the dish. Trim off any excess and crimp the rim. Brush with egg and sprinkle with flaked salt. Cut a 3cm (1¼in) slit in the lid for steam to escape.

8 Preheat the air fryer to 180°C/350°F for 3 minutes.

9 Cook at 180°C/350°F for 35–40 minutes until golden brown. Let cool for 10 minutes before serving.

Prep + cook time
2 hours
Serves 4–6

HONEYED FIG & RICOTTA FILO PARCELS

6 sheets of filo pastry, defrosted
   if frozen
60g (½ stick) unsalted butter, melted
120g (½ cup) ricotta
4 tbsp fig jam
2 tbsp honey
to serve: figs, honey, and
   toasted nuts

1 Lay out one sheet of filo pastry on the work surface, brush generously with melted butter, then fold in half like a book.

2 Dollop one-sixth of the ricotta and jam in the bottom left-hand corner, leaving a 3cm (1¼in) border from the edge of the pastry. Fold the bottom right-hand corner over the filling to create a triangle shape, pressing down the pastry with the edges of your hands to seal the filling inside. Finally, fold the pastry upwards to create another layer and then again until you have a triangular parcel.

3 Brush the outside of the parcel with melted butter and set aside. Continue the process until you have all six parcels.

4 Preheat the air fryer to 180°C/350°F for 3 minutes.

5 Place the parcels directly in the air fryer basket and bake at 180°C/350°F for 12–15 minutes, or until evenly golden brown.

6 Leave to cool for 5 minutes before serving with fresh figs, a drizzle of honey, and some toasted nuts.

SERVE IT These are best eaten fresh!

Prep + cook time
1 hour
Makes 6

SPICED PUMPKIN PIES

225g (8oz) canned pumpkin
100g (½ cup) light soft brown sugar
1 large (US extra large) egg
½ tbsp cornflour (cornstarch)
1 tsp ground cinnamon
1 tsp ground ginger
½ tsp allspice
½ tsp ground black pepper
½ tsp salt
to serve: crème fraîche and
   maple syrup

BISCUIT BASE:
250g (9oz) caramelized biscuits
   (cookies), crushed
½ tsp salt
100g (7 tbsp) salted butter, melted

1 Place the pumpkin, sugar, egg, cornflour, cinnamon, ginger, allspice, pepper, and salt into a mixing bowl, then beat with a wooden spoon until fully combined. Set aside while you make the biscuit base.
2 Place the biscuits inside a sealed food bag and bash with a rolling pin until they resemble a fine sandy crumb. Alternatively, you can place these into a blender and pulse. Tip the biscuit crumbs into a small mixing bowl, then add the salt and melted butter. Mix well with a spoon until all the crumbs are coated and the butter is absorbed.
3 Divide the biscuit base mixture amongst six loose-bottomed fluted metal tart cases (10–12.5cm/4–5in in diameter). Using the back of a small spoon, press the crumbs to create a crust (shell) about 5mm (¼in) thick, pressing it up the sides and into the edges.

4 Preheat the air fryer to 160°C/325°F for 3 minutes.
5 Bake at 160°C/325°F for 5 minutes. The bases will puff up while baking, so remove from the air fryer basket and push the bases down with the back of a spoon.
6 Divide the pumpkin filling evenly amongst the six tarts. Smooth the top of the pies before placing back in the air fryer and baking for a further 10 minutes at 160°C/325°F.
7 Leave to cool completely on a wire rack, then pop the tarts out of their cases. Serve with a dollop of crème fraîche and a drizzle of maple syrup.

KEEP IT These will keep for up to 3 days in the fridge.

Prep + cook time
30 minutes
Makes 6

PISTACHIO & ORANGE BLOSSOM BAKLAVA

(VEGAN)

200g (1⅔ cup) pistachios, plus extra
    crushed pistachios to decorate
100g (generous ¾ cup) pecans
    or walnuts
40g (2¼ tbsp) honey
grated zest of 1 orange
1 tsp sea salt
200g (7oz) dairy-free butter, melted
270g (9½oz) filo pastry sheets,
    defrosted if frozen

SYRUP:
150g (¾ cup) golden caster
    (superfine) sugar
juice of 1 orange
1 tsp ground cinnamon

TIP The baklava can be eaten straight away once cool, but is best left to set overnight in the fridge.

1 Place all the nuts in a food processor and pulse to a coarse sand. Place in a mixing bowl with the honey, orange zest, and sea salt. Mix and set aside.
2 Brush a 20cm (8in) brownie tin with melted butter. Brush a sheet of pastry edge to edge with butter. Lay it in the tin, pressing it into the corners. Butter another sheet and layer the opposite way. Repeat the process, alternating layers, until you've used six sheets.
3 Fill the lined tin with the nut filling, pressing the filling down until it's compacted. Using scissors, trim off any overhanging pastry and fold over any extra edges inwards.
4 Cut the remaining sheets of filo pastry into 20cm (8in) squares. Brush each sheet with butter and layer on top of the nut filling, pressing down firmly.
5 Brush the top layer with the remaining butter.

6 Take a small sharp knife and score six diagonal lines into the pastry, then six vertical lines to create the classic diamond shape.
7 Preheat the air fryer to 160°C/325°F for 3 minutes.
8 Put in the air fryer basket and bake at 160°C/325°F for 10 minutes, then cover with foil and cook at 140°C/280°F for 25 minutes.
9 Meanwhile, combine the syrup ingredients and 3½ tablespoons water in a small pan, bring to a simmer, and cook for 5 minutes until it coats the back of a spoon.
10 While hot, cover the baklava with the syrup. Top with extra crushed pistachios and place on a wire rack to cool completely in the tin.

KEEP IT This will keep for up to 2 weeks in an airtight container.

Prep + cook time
1 hour, plus setting
Serves 18

PLUM & BLACKBERRY PIES

8 ripe plums
150g (generous 1 cup) blackberries
grated zest and juice of 1 lemon
100g (½ cup) golden caster
    (superfine) sugar
1 tbsp cornflour (cornstarch)
1 egg, beaten
2 tbsp caster (superfine) sugar
to serve: whipped cream

PASTRY:
120g (1 stick) unsalted butter,
    softened
80g (½ cup plus 1 tbsp) icing
    (confectioners') sugar
1 egg, beaten
½ tsp vanilla paste
½ tsp salt
200g (1½ cups) plain (all-purpose)
    flour, plus extra for dusting

1 Preheat the air fryer to 200°C/400°F for 3 minutes.
2 Remove the stones (pits) from the plums and cut them into sixths. Put in a bowl with the blackberries, lemon zest and juice, sugar, and cornflour, and combine. Transfer to a heatproof dish.
3 Place in the air fryer and bake at 200°C/400°F for 15 minutes, stirring every 5 minutes. Transfer to a metal tray to cool quickly. Cover with clingfilm to stop a skin from forming.
4 To make the pastry, in a mixing bowl, beat the softened butter with the icing sugar, then add the egg, vanilla paste, and salt, and stir until combined. Sift in the flour and stir until a soft dough forms and the flour is absorbed. Wrap in clingfilm, flatten into a disc, and place in the fridge to chill for 1 hour. At the same time, place the cooled fruit filling in the fridge to chill fully, too.

5 On a floured surface, roll out the pastry to 1cm (½in) thick. Cut out 12 discs with a 10cm (4in) round cutter. Put on a lined baking sheet and chill for 15 minutes.
6 Divide the filling amongst six of the discs, piling it in a mound. Brush the edges with egg, then place another disc of pastry on top. Using a flour-dusted fork, seal the edges. Use the pastry ring to trim off any scraggly edges.
7 Brush with egg, sprinkle with the caster sugar, and cut a 1cm (½in) hole in the top for steam to escape.
8 Preheat the air fryer to 180°C/350°F for 3 minutes and line the basket with baking parchment.
9 Put the pastries in the lined basket and bake at 180°C/350°F for 25 minutes until golden.
10 Let cool for 10 minutes before serving with cream.

**Prep + cook time
2 hours
Makes 6**

PEAR & GINGER STRUDEL (VEGAN)

500g (1lb 2oz) pears, cored and cubed

50g (1¾oz) stem ginger, finely chopped

50g (¼ cup) golden caster (superfine) sugar

40g (generous ¼ cup) raisins

1 tsp ground cinnamon

30g (6 tsp) dairy-free butter, softened, plus 75g (¾ stick), melted

40g (¾ cup) breadcrumbs

6 sheets of filo pastry, defrosted if frozen

to serve: icing (confectioners') sugar and ice cream

1 Preheat the air fryer to 180°C/350°F for 3 minutes.
2 Combine the pears, ginger, sugar, raisins, cinnamon, and 20g (4 tsp) butter in a mixing bowl. Pour into a heatproof dish and bake at 180°C/350°F for 10 minutes, stirring halfway through. Set aside to cool on a wire rack.
3 Turn the heat up to 200°C/400°F. Combine the breadcrumbs and 10g (2 tsp) butter in a heatproof dish, and bake at 200°C/400°F stirring every minute until evenly golden. Set aside to cool on a wire rack.
4 Take one sheet of pastry and brush with melted butter. Take another sheet and layer 10cm (4in) of it over the buttered sheet to create one longer length. Brush generously with butter, then layer another sheet over the first piece, then another over the second until you've used all six sheets.

5 Combine the filling with the breadcrumbs. Spoon the filling in a sausage-like length, 10cm (4in) from the top edge of the pastry, leaving 5cm (2in) of pastry at each end. Fold the ends of the pastry inwards to encase the filling. Taking the top edge of the pastry, roll downwards to create a long sausage. Then roll the pastry into a swirl.
6 Preheat the air fryer to 180°C/350°F for 3 minutes.
7 Put the swirl into a greased 20cm (8in) round tin. Brush with any remaining melted butter and bake at 180°C/350°F for 25–35 minutes until golden brown.
8 Let cool for 15 minutes, then remove from the tin. Dust with icing sugar and serve with ice cream.

KEEP IT It keeps for 5 days in an airtight container in the fridge.

Prep + cook time
1 hour
Serves 8

APPLE PIES

4 eating apples, peeled and cubed
juice of 1 lemon
100g (½ cup) caster (superfine)
    sugar
1½ tbsp cornflour (cornstarch)
30g (2 tbsp) unsalted butter,
    softened
2 tsp ground cinnamon
4 tbsp granulated sugar
320g (11oz) sheet of puff pastry
plain (all-purpose) flour, for dusting
1 egg, beaten

1 Preheat the air fryer to 160°C/325°F for 3 minutes.
2 Combine the apples, lemon juice, caster sugar, cornflour, butter, and 1 teaspoon cinnamon in a heatproof dish.
3 Place in the air fryer basket and bake at 160°C/325°F for 10 minutes, stirring halfway through. Turn the setting up to 200°C/400°F for 5 minutes to activate the cornflour and thicken the compote, stirring again halfway through and again at the end. Cover the compote with clingfilm to stop a skin from forming, and place on a wire rack to cool completely.
4 While the compote is cooling, combine the remaining 1 teaspoon cinnamon with the granulated sugar in a small bowl, and set aside.
5 Unroll the pastry on a lightly floured work surface. Cut it into eight equal rectangles.

6 Divide the compote amongst four of the pastry pieces, spooning it into the centre of each rectangle and leaving a 2cm (¾in) border around the edge. Brush with egg, then top with another rectangle of pastry, gently placing it on top, stretching it over the compote and sealing it around the filling using the sides of your hands.
7 Crimp the edges with a fork, then trim with a knife. Cut a 1cm (½in) slit in the centre to allow steam to escape. Brush all over with beaten egg and sprinkle with the cinnamon sugar.
8 Preheat the air fryer to 180°C/350°F for 3 minutes and line the basket with baking parchment.
9 Bake two pies at a time at 180°C/350°F for 16–20 minutes until crisp and golden. Let cool for 10 minutes before serving.

Prep + cook time
1 hour
Makes 4

DOUGHS

There is no getting away from the fact that making dough can be time-consuming. However, once you've made and proved your dough, cooking it in an air fryer means your springy breads and sweet, sticky rolls can be ready to enjoy in much less time than when using an oven.

HOTDOG ROLLS WITH MUSTARD MAYO DIP

1½ tsp active dried yeast
150ml (⅔ cup) full-fat (whole) milk, lukewarm, plus extra for brushing
300g (2 cups plus 2 tbsp) strong white bread flour, plus extra for dusting
2 tsp caster (superfine) sugar
1 tsp salt
1 large (US extra large) egg, beaten
50g (3½ tbsp) unsalted butter, softened
420g (15oz) jar hotdogs (8 sausages)
4 large gherkin slices, cut in half lengthways
1 tbsp poppy seeds

DIP:
1 small shallot, finely chopped
5 tbsp mayonnaise
2 tsp English (hot) mustard
1 tsp tomato ketchup
1 tsp horseradish
1 tbsp roughly chopped dill
½ tsp ground black pepper

1 Sprinkle the yeast over the lukewarm milk. Let sit for 2 minutes until foaming.
2 Tip the flour, sugar, and salt into a mixing bowl or a stand mixer fitted with a dough hook. Add the egg and yeasted milk. Stir until a dough starts to form.
3 Knead for 6 minutes, then add the butter, and knead for 5 minutes until smooth and elastic. Put into an oiled bowl, cover with clingfilm, and leave in a warm place for 1–2 hours until doubled in size.
4 Knead on a floured surface for 1 minute, then split the dough into eight portions, 70g (2½oz) each. Roll each portion of dough into a ball, using your hand in the shape of a claw and rolling the dough in circles. Cover the other balls with a tea towel while you work.
5 Cut eight 10cm (4in) squares of parchment. Dust each dough ball with flour and roll into a rectangle, the length of the hotdogs and 8cm (3¼in) wide.

6 Place a halved gherkin slice and a hotdog in the centre of each piece of dough, then pinch the dough together. Place on a square of parchment and then onto a baking tray. Cover with a tea towel and leave for 30 minutes, or until doubled in size.
7 Preheat the air fryer to 180°C/350°F for 3 minutes.
8 Brush the rolls with milk and sprinkle with the poppy seeds. Use the parchment to lift them into the preheated air fryer. Bake at 180°C/350°F for 12 minutes, or until a deep golden brown.
9 Meanwhile, make the dip by combining all the ingredients in a bowl and seasoning to taste.
10 Serve the warm hot dog rolls with the dip!

KEEP IT Store in an airtight container in the fridge for 3 days. Reheat in the air fryer.

Prep + cook time
3 hours
Makes 8

CHEESY GARLIC DOUGH BALLS

1½ tsp active dried yeast
130ml (½ cup plus 2 tsp) full-fat (whole) milk, lukewarm
250g (1¾ cups) strong white bread flour, plus extra for dusting
2 tsp caster (superfine) sugar
1 tsp salt
1 egg, beaten
40g (3 tbsp) unsalted butter, softened
20g (½ cup) panko breadcrumbs
150g (5½oz) pre-grated mozzarella

GARLIC BUTTER:
100g (7 tbsp) salted butter, softened
4 garlic cloves, minced
2 tbsp roughly chopped parsley

1 Sprinkle the yeast over the lukewarm milk. Let sit for 2 minutes until foaming.
2 Tip the flour, sugar, and salt into a mixing bowl or stand mixer with a dough hook. Add the beaten egg and yeasted milk. Combine with a wooden spoon until a dough starts to form.
3 Knead for 6 minutes, then add the softened butter and knead for a further 5 minutes until smooth and elastic. Put into an oiled bowl, cover with clingfilm, and leave in a warm place for 1–2 hours, or until doubled in size.
4 Meanwhile, grease the inside of a 20cm (8in) round tin with butter, then coat with the breadcrumbs.
5 Mix together the garlic butter ingredients to combine, then set aside.
6 Knead the dough for 1 minute, then weigh it out into 18 portions, about 30g (1oz) each.

7 Roll each portion into a dough ball, taking your hand in the shape of claw and rolling the dough in circular motions on the work surface.
8 Place all the dough balls into the breadcrumbed tin, leaving a 1cm (½in) gap between them. Sprinkle the grated mozzarella between all the gaps. Cover the tin with clingfilm and leave the buns to prove for 30–45 minutes, or until doubled in size.
9 Preheat the air fryer to 180°C/350°F for 3 minutes.
10 Place into the preheated air fryer basket and bake for 20 minutes at 180°C/350°F until deep golden brown.
11 Melt the garlic parsley butter and brush it over the dough balls, then serve immediately.

**Prep + cook time
3 hours
Makes 18**

CHORIZO, PEPPER & MANCHEGO FOCACCIA

2 tsp active dried yeast

300ml (1¼ cups) lukewarm water

350g (2½ cups) strong white bread flour, plus extra for dusting

2 tsp caster (superfine) sugar

1 tsp salt

4 tbsp extra virgin olive oil

100g (3½oz) chorizo, chopped

80g (2½oz) guindilla peppers

1 tsp flaked sea salt

50g (scant ½ cup) grated Manchego or Parmesan

1 Sprinkle the yeast over the lukewarm milk. Let sit for 2 minutes until foaming.

2 Place the flour, sugar, and salt in a mixing bowl or a stand mixer fitted with a dough hook. Add the yeasted water, and stir with a wooden spoon until a shaggy dough forms.

3 Knead the dough for 5–8 minutes until the dough becomes smooth and elastic. Place in an oiled bowl, cover with cling film, and set aside in a warm spot for 1 hour, or until doubled in size.

4 Once the dough has doubled in sized, turn it out onto a lightly floured work surface and knead for 1 minute to knock out the air.

5 Lightly oil your hands and a deep 20cm (8in) tin, then transfer the dough to the tin. Stretch the dough to fill three-quarters of the tin. Cover and set aside again for 1 hour, or until doubled in size.

6 The dough should be bubbly and jiggle when the tin is gently shaken. Drizzle with 3 tablespoons olive oil, then dimple the dough all over using your oiled fingertips. Sprinkle with the chopped chorizo, guindilla peppers, and flaked sea salt.

7 Preheat the air fryer to 200°C/400°F for 3 minutes.

8 Place in the preheated air fryer basket and cook at 200°C/400°F for 15–18 minutes, or until the crust is golden brown.

9 Let cool for 15 minutes before removing from the tin to cool completely.

10 Place the focaccia on a board, then sprinkle all over with the grated cheese, and drizzle over the remaining olive oil. Serve in thick slices.

KEEP IT It will keep for up to 3 days in an airtight container.

Prep + cook time
2 hours 45 minutes
Serves 6

MOZZARELLA & MEATBALL CALZONES

¼ tsp active dried yeast

150–175ml (⅔–¾ cup) lukewarm water

250g (1¾ cups) strong white bread flour, plus extra for dusting

½ tsp caster (superfine) sugar

½ tsp salt

FILLING:

1 shallot, finely chopped

12 small meatballs

2 tbsp olive oil, plus extra for drizzling

½ tsp fine sea salt

½ tsp ground black pepper

200g (7oz) passata (strained tomatoes)

1 garlic clove, finely chopped

1 sprig of basil

100g (scant 1 cup) pre-grated mozzarella

1 Sprinkle the yeast over the lukewarm milk. Let sit for 2 minutes until foaming.

2 Place the flour, sugar, and salt in a large mixing bowl or a stand mixer with a dough hook. Add the yeasted water, and stir with a wooden spoon until a shaggy dough forms.

3 Knead for 5–8 minutes until smooth and elastic. Place in an oiled bowl, cover with clingfilm, and set aside in a warm spot for 1 hour (it will rise a bit, but not double in size).

4 Preheat the air fryer to 200°C/400°F for 3 minutes.

5 For the filling, combine the shallot, meatballs, oil, and seasoning in a heatproof dish. Bake in the air fryer at 200°C/400°F for 5 minutes. Stir in the passata and garlic, then submerge the basil in the sauce. Bake for 10 minutes at 180°C/350°F, then place on a wire rack to cool.

6 Once the meatballs are cool and the dough has proved, on a floured surface, cut the dough into four pieces. Roll each piece into a 15cm (6in) circle.

7 Place three meatballs, a tablespoon of sauce, and one-quarter of the mozzarella in the centre of each circle. Lift the two edges to meet in the middle, then pinch all the way along to seal in the filling. Cut a 1cm (½in) slit in the centre to allow steam to escape.

8 Preheat the air fryer to 180°C/350°F for 3 minutes.

9 Put in the air fryer basket, drizzle with olive oil, then bake at 180°C/350°F for 12 minutes, or until golden brown. Let cool in the basket for a few minutes, then cool on a wire rack for 10 minutes before serving.

Prep + cook time

2 hours

Makes 4

FETA & HOT HONEY SWIRLS

½ tsp active dried yeast

130ml (½ cup plus 2 tsp) full-fat (whole) milk, lukewarm, plus extra for brushing

250g (1¾ cups) strong white bread flour, plus extra for dusting

2 tsp caster (superfine) sugar

1 tsp sea salt

1 egg, beaten

40g (3 tbsp) unsalted butter, softened

100g (3½oz) feta, crumbled

SPICED BUTTER:

100g (7 tbsp) unsalted butter, softened

20g (4 tsp) honey

1 tsp chilli flakes

1 tsp dried oregano

1 tsp dried thyme

1 tsp sea salt

1 tsp ground black pepper

1 Sprinkle the yeast over the lukewarm milk. Let sit for 2 minutes until foaming.
2 Place the flour, sugar, and salt in a large mixing bowl or a stand mixer with a dough hook. Add the yeasted milk and beaten egg, and stir with a wooden spoon until a dough forms.
3 Knead for 6 minutes, then add the butter and knead for 5 minutes until smooth and elastic. Place in an oiled bowl, cover with clingfilm, and set aside in a warm spot for 1 hour, or until doubled in size.
4 Meanwhile, combine the spiced butter ingredients, and set aside.
5 Knead the dough for 1 minute to knock out the air. Dust lightly with flour, then roll out into a 30 x 20cm (12 x 8in) rectangle.
6 Spread two-thirds of the spiced butter on the dough, spreading it from edge to edge, using the back of a spoon, then sprinkle over the crumbled feta.

7 Taking a long edge of the dough, roll it into a tight swirl. Cut it into six equal pieces. Place each piece, swirl-side down, in a greased metal pudding tin.
8 Place the pudding tins on a baking tray and cover again with clingfilm. Set aside for 30 minutes to prove in a warm place, or until doubled in size.
9 Preheat the air fryer to 180°C/350°F for 3 minutes.
10 Brush with milk, then place in the preheated air fryer basket and bake for 12 minutes at 180°C/350°F, or until a deep golden brown.
11 Brush with the rest of the butter and place on a wire rack to cool in the tins for 10 minutes, then turn out and serve warm.

KEEP IT These will keep for up to 3 days in an airtight container in the fridge.

Prep + cook time
2 hours
Makes 6

CHOCOLATE ORANGE BABKA

2 tsp active dried yeast
175ml (¾ cup) full-fat (whole) milk, lukewarm, plus extra for brushing
400g (3 cups) plain (all-purpose) flour, plus extra for dusting
20g (5 tsp) caster (superfine) sugar
grated zest of 1 large orange
1 tsp salt
2 large (US extra large) eggs
30g (2 tbsp) unsalted butter, softened
½ tsp salt

FILLING:
60g (½ stick) unsalted butter
100g (3½oz) dark (bittersweet) chocolate, chopped
4 tbsp unsweetened cocoa powder
30g (2½ tbsp) soft brown sugar

SYRUP:
80g (6½ tbsp) caster (superfine) sugar
juice of 1 large orange

1 Sprinkle the yeast over the lukewarm milk. Let sit for 2 minutes until foaming.
2 Tip the flour, sugar, zest, and salt into a mixing bowl or stand mixer with a dough hook. Add the egg and yeasted milk, and stir with a wooden spoon until a dough starts to form.
3 Knead for 6 minutes, then add the butter and knead for 5 minutes until smooth and elastic. Put into an oiled bowl, cover with clingfilm, and leave in a warm place for 1–2 hours until doubled in size.
4 Meanwhile, put the filling ingredients into a small pan over a low heat and stir until melted. Set aside.
5 Put the syrup ingredients and 3½ tablespoons water into a small pan and simmer on a medium heat for 10 minutes until it coats the spoon. Set aside.
6 Knead the dough for 1 minute, then roll out on a floured surface into a 30 x 25cm (12 x 10in) rectangle.

7 Spread the chocolate filling from edge to edge, coating the whole piece of dough. Taking a long edge, roll it into a tight swirl. Cut the roll in half lengthways into two long pieces.
8 Place the two pieces next to each other, cut-side up and overlap them like a plait (braid). Gently lift the plait into a greased 20cm (8in) loose-bottomed tin, cut-side up. Cover with clingfilm and leave in a warm place for 1–2 hours until doubled in size.
9 Preheat the air fryer to 170°C/340°F for 3 minutes.
10 Brush the dough with milk, put in the preheated air fryer basket, and cook at 170°C/340°F for 30 minutes until golden.
11 Brush with the orange syrup while hot. Cool completely in the tin.

**Prep + cook time
3 hours
Serves 8–10**

TAHINI, MAPLE & PECAN BUNS

1½ tsp instant dried yeast
130ml (½ cup plus 2 tsp) full-fat
   (whole) milk, lukewarm
250g (1¾ cups) strong white bread
   flour, plus extra for dusting
20g (5 tsp) caster (superfine) sugar
grated zest of 1 lime, plus extra
   to decorate
½ tsp salt
1 egg, beaten
40g (3 tbsp) unsalted butter,
   softened

FILLING:
50g (3½ tbsp) unsalted butter,
   softened
25g (2 tbsp) soft brown sugar
50g (¼ cup) tahini
25g (1¼ tbsp) maple syrup
75g (¾ cup) pecan halves, roughly
   chopped, plus extra to decorate
1 tsp flaked sea salt

ICING:
100g (¾ cup) icing (confectioners')
   sugar
25g (1¼ tbsp) maple syrup
juice of 1 lime

1 Sprinkle the yeast over the lukewarm milk. Let sit for 2 minutes until foaming.
2 Tip the flour, sugar, lime zest, and salt into a mixing bowl or stand mixer with a dough hook. Add the egg and yeasted milk. Combine with a wooden spoon until a dough starts to form.
3 Knead for 6 minutes, then add the butter and knead for 5 minutes until smooth and elastic. Put into an oiled bowl, cover with clingfilm, and leave in a warm place for 1–2 hours until doubled in size.
4 Meanwhile, for the filling, place the softened butter, sugar, tahini, and maple syrup in a mixing bowl, and beat until combined. Set aside at room temperature (you want the filling to be spreadable, so don't put it in the fridge).
5 Once proved, knead the dough on a lightly floured work surface for 1 minute. Roll out into a 30 x 25cm (12 x 10in) rectangle.

6 Spread the soft butter filling from edge to edge, then sprinkle with the roughly chopped pecans and sea salt.
7 Taking a long edge of the dough, roll it into a tight swirl. Cut it into six equal pieces. Place each piece, swirl-side down, in a greased metal pudding tin. Set aside to prove for 30 minutes, or until doubled in size.
8 Preheat the air fryer to 180°C/350°F for 3 minutes.
9 Place in the air fryer basket and bake at 180°C/350°F for 12 minutes until deep golden.
10 For the icing, sift the icing sugar into a bowl, and stir in the maple syrup and lime juice until smooth.
11 Brush the buns all over with the icing while still warm, then sprinkle with extra pecans and lime zest to decorate.

Prep + cook time
2 hours 30 minutes
Makes 6

LEMON CURD & POPPY SEED SWIRLS

1½ tsp active dried yeast
130ml (½ cup plus 2 tsp) full-fat (whole) milk, lukewarm
250g (1¾ cups) strong white bread flour, plus extra for dusting
20g (5 tsp) caster (superfine) sugar
grated zest of 1 lemon
3 tbsp poppy seeds
½ tsp salt
1 large (US extra large) egg, beaten
40g (3 tbsp) unsalted butter, softened
150g (5½oz) lemon curd

ICING:
100g (¾ cup) icing (confectioners') sugar, sifted
juice of 1 lemon
1 tbsp poppy seeds

1 Sprinkle the yeast over the lukewarm milk. Let sit for 2 minutes until foaming.
2 Tip the flour, sugar, lemon zest, poppy seeds, and salt into a mixing bowl or stand mixer with a dough hook. Add the egg and yeasted milk. Combine with a wooden spoon until a dough starts to form.
3 Knead for 6 minutes, then add the butter and knead for 5 minutes until smooth and elastic. Put into an oiled bowl, cover with clingfilm, and leave in a warm place for 1–2 hours until doubled in size.
4 Once proved, knead the dough on a lightly floured work surface for 1 minute. Roll out into a 30 x 25cm (12 x 10in) rectangle.
5 Spread the lemon curd from edge to edge over the whole piece of dough.
6 Taking a long edge of the dough, roll it into a tight swirl. Cut the swirl into six equal pieces.
7 Place each piece, swirl-side down, in a greased metal pudding tin.
8 Cover with clingfilm and leave to prove for 30 minutes, or until doubled in size.
9 Once proved, preheat the air fryer to 180°C/350°F for 3 minutes.
10 Place the buns in the preheated air fryer and cook at 180°C/350°F for 12 minutes.
11 Meanwhile, combine the icing ingredients in a bowl and mix until smooth.
12 Remove the buns from the air fryer and leave to cool for 5 minutes, then brush generously with icing while still warm.

KEEP IT Keep for up to 3 days in an airtight container.

**Prep + cook time
2 hours 30 minutes
Makes 6**

APPLE CRUMBLE BUNS

½ tsp instant dried yeast

130ml (½ cup plus 2 tsp) full-fat (whole) milk, lukewarm, plus extra for brushing

250g (1¾ cups) strong white bread flour, plus extra for dusting

1 tsp ground cinnamon

20g (5 tsp) caster (superfine) sugar

½ tsp sea salt

1 egg, beaten

1 tsp vanilla extract

40g (3 tbsp) unsalted butter, softened

FILLING:

2 apples, cored and cut into 5mm (¼in) chunks

20g (1½ tbsp) unsalted butter

1 tbsp caster (superfine) sugar

1 tsp ground cinnamon

150ml (⅔ cup) store-bought custard

CRUMBLE:

30g (2 tbsp) unsalted butter, cold and cubed

40g (5 tbsp) plain (all-purpose) flour

20g (5 tsp) sugar

1 tsp flaked sea salt

1 Sprinkle the yeast over the lukewarm milk. Let sit for 2 minutes until foaming.

2 Put the flour, cinnamon, sugar, and salt in a mixing bowl or a stand mixer with a dough hook. Add the egg, vanilla, and yeasted milk. Stir with a wooden spoon until a dough forms.

3 Knead for 6 minutes, add the butter, and knead for 5 minutes until smooth and elastic. Place in an oiled bowl, cover with clingfilm, and set aside for 1 hour until doubled in size.

4 Preheat the air fryer to 180°C/350°F for 3 minutes.

5 For the filling, mix the apples, butter, sugar, and cinnamon in a heatproof dish. Place in the air fryer basket and bake at 180°C/350°F for 10–15 minutes until softened and starting to caramelize. Let cool.

6 For the crumble, rub the cold butter into the flour using your fingertips until it is a sandy consistency. Stir in the sugar and salt. Set aside.

7 Cut six 10cm (4in) squares of parchment.

8 Knead the dough for 1 minute, then divide it into six pieces. Shape into balls, using your hand in a claw shape while rolling in circles. Place each ball onto a square of parchment. Lightly dust with flour, then flatten the balls and press a dip in the centre using your fingers. Fill each dip with 1 tablespoon custard.

9 Place on a baking tray, cover with oiled clingfilm, and prove for 30 minutes until doubled in size.

10 Preheat the air fryer to 180°C/350°F for 3 minutes.

11 Brush with milk, then divide the filling amongst the buns. Sprinkle with the crumble. Place in a preheated air fryer basket using the paper, and bake for 10 minutes at 180°C/350°F until golden brown.

12 Let cool before serving.

Prep + cook time
2 hours 30 minutes
Makes 6

CINNAMON BUNS (VEGAN)

½ tsp instant dried yeast
150ml (⅔ cup) oat milk or
   alternative, lukewarm
250g (1¾ cups) strong white bread
   flour, plus extra for dusting
20g (5 tsp) caster (superfine) sugar
½ tsp sea salt
50g (1¾oz) dairy-free butter,
   softened

FILLING:
100g (3½oz) dairy-free butter,
   softened
100g (½ cup) light soft brown sugar
1 tbsp ground cinnamon
1 tsp flaked sea salt

ICING:
200g (1½ cups) icing (confectioners')
   sugar
juice of 1 lemon
1 tsp ground cinnamon

1 Sprinkle the yeast over the lukewarm milk. Let sit for 2 minutes until foaming.
2 Place the flour, sugar, and salt in a mixing bowl or a stand mixer fitted with a dough hook. Add the yeasted milk and stir with a wooden spoon until a shaggy dough forms.
3 Knead for 6 minutes, then add the butter and knead for 5 minutes until smooth and elastic. Place in an oiled bowl, cover with clingfilm, and set aside in a warm spot for 1 hour, or until doubled in size.
4 Meanwhile, combine all the filling ingredients in a small bowl to make the cinnamon butter. Set aside.
5 For the icing, sift the icing sugar into a bowl, then stir in the lemon juice and cinnamon. It should be smooth and thick.
6 Turn the dough out onto a lightly floured work surface and knead for 1 minute to knock out the air.

7 Roll out into a 30 x 20cm (12 x 8in) rectangle. Spread the cinnamon butter from edge to edge over the whole piece of dough.
8 Taking a long edge of the dough, roll it into a tight swirl. Cut the swirl into four equal pieces.
9 Place the buns swirl-side down in greased metal pudding tins.
10 Preheat the air fryer to 180°C/350°F for 3 minutes.
11 Bake the buns in the preheated air fryer basket for 10–12 minutes at 180°C/350°F until deep golden brown, but with a soft doughy centre.
12 Cool in the tins on a wire rack for 10 minutes, then flip out of the tins while still warm and brush generously with the icing. Leave to cool for another 10 minutes, then enjoy while still warm.

Prep + cook time
2 hours
Makes 4

PISTACHIO & ROSE BUNS

½ tsp active dried yeast

130ml (½ cup plus 2 tsp) full-fat (whole) milk, lukewarm, plus extra for brushing

250g (1¾ cups) strong white bread flour, plus extra for dusting

½ tsp ground cardamom

grated zest of 1 large orange

½ tsp sea salt

1 egg, beaten

20g (4 tsp) honey

40g (3 tbsp) unsalted butter, softened

FILLING:

100g (generous ¾ cup) pistachios, plus extra pistachios, chopped, to decorate

75g (¾ stick) unsalted butter, softened

40g (2½ tbsp) honey

1 tsp flaked sea salt

GLAZE:

juice of 1 large orange

30g (2½ tbsp) caster (superfine) sugar

½ tbsp dried rose petals, or 2 tsp rose water

1 Sprinkle the yeast over the lukewarm milk. Let sit for 2 minutes until foaming.
2 Place the flour in a large bowl or a stand mixer fitted with a dough hook. Add the cardamom, orange zest, and salt, and mix for 30 seconds until combined. Add the yeasted milk, beaten egg, and honey. Mix with a wooden spoon until a dough starts to form.
3 Knead for 6 minutes, add the butter, and knead for 5 minutes until smooth and elastic. Put into an oiled bowl, cover with clingfilm, and leave in a warm spot for 1 hour until doubled in size.
4 Meanwhile, for the filling, grind the pistachios in a food processor or blender until like coarse sand, then combine with the butter, honey, and salt. Set aside.
5 Mix the glaze ingredients and 2 tablespoons water in a pan. Simmer for 5 minutes until it coats the back of a spoon.

6 Knead the dough for 1 minute, then roll out into a 40 x 20cm (16 x 8in) rectangle. Spread the pistachio butter from edge to edge.
7 Taking a long edge of the dough, roll it into a tight swirl. Cut it into six equal pieces and place in a greased 20cm (8in) square tin, leaving 2.5cm (1in) between each bun.
8 Cover with clingfilm and leave in a warm place for 30 minutes, or until doubled in size.
9 Preheat the air fryer to 180°C/350°F for 3 minutes.
10 Brush the buns with milk, then bake in the preheated air fryer at 180°C/350°F for 12 minutes until golden.
11 Let cool on a wire rack for 10 minutes, then brush with the glaze and sprinkle with chopped pistachios. Let cool.

**Prep + cook time
2 hours 15 minutes
Makes 6**

PUDDINGS

Use your air fryer for fuss-free desserts, saving yourself time and energy when you want to whip up a pud. The efficient heat of the air fryer creates wonderfully crisp crumble and cobbler toppings, but you can even bake meringues to perfection by using a lower temperature.

MANGO & LIME CHEESECAKE

600g (2⅔ cups) full-fat cream
   cheese
125g (½ cup plus 2 tbsp) caster
   (superfine) sugar
2 tbsp cornflour (cornstarch)
1 large (US extra large) egg
150ml (⅔ cup) double (heavy) cream
grated zest of 1 lime, plus extra
   to decorate

BASE:
180g (6½oz) digestives (graham
   crackers), crumbed
80g (¾ stick) salted butter, melted

MANGO JELLY:
2 sheets of gelatine
255g (8oz) canned mango in syrup
   (drained weight from 425g/15oz
   can), plus 2 tbsp syrup from
   the can

1 For the base, combine the biscuit crumbs and melted butter, then press into a 20cm (8in) round loose-bottom tin in an even layer. Place in the fridge while you make the filling.
2 Whisk the cream cheese, sugar, cornflour, and egg in a mixing bowl until smooth. Add the cream and lime zest, then whisk again until it is the consistency of softly whipped cream.
3 Preheat the air fryer to 160°C/325°F for 3 minutes.
4 Pour the filling into the tin on top of the base, smooth with the back of a spoon, then tap the tin on the work surface to knock out any air bubbles. Place in the air fryer basket and bake at 160°C/325°F for 35 minutes until it has a light golden top, and is firm, but still has a wobble.
5 Cool completely in the tin on a wire rack, then put in the fridge for at least 2 hours.

6 Once the cheesecake is chilled, you can make the jelly. Soak the gelatine in cold water and set aside.
7 Put the drained mango and the syrup into a blender, and blend to a purée. Heat in a small pan over a low heat for 1–2 minutes until just hot (you should be able to touch it; if you overheat the purée, let it cool a little).
8 Remove the softened gelatine sheets from the cold water and place in the warmed purée. Stir to dissolve, then set aside to cool for 10 minutes.
9 Once cool, pour on top of the cheesecake. Chill in the fridge overnight.
10 To help the cheesecake out of the tin, soak a cloth in hot water, and apply to the sides of the tin. Push the base out, then slide the cheesecake onto a plate. Decorate with lime zest.

**Prep + cook time
1 hour, plus chilling
Serves 6–8**

SAUCY SALTED CARAMEL PUDS

140g (1¼ sticks) unsalted butter, softened
140g (scant ¾ cup) dark soft brown sugar
2 large (US extra large) eggs, beaten
1 tsp vanilla paste
1 tsp fine salt
140g (1 cup) plain (all-purpose) flour, plus extra for dusting
2 tbsp store-bought salted caramel (firm set)
to serve: salted caramel ice cream

1 Combine the softened butter and sugar in a medium mixing bowl, and beat with a wooden spoon until the mixture lightens. Add the eggs, vanilla paste, and salt, and beat for a minute, then sift in the flour. Fold the flour through until the batter is smooth.

2 Preheat the air fryer to 180°C/350°F for 3 minutes.

3 Grease four metal pudding tins and dust with flour. Divide half the mixture amongst the metal pudding tins, smoothing it with the back of a spoon to create a flat layer. Create a dip in the centre for the caramel sauce to sit in.

4 Spoon ½ tablespoon caramel sauce into each tin. Divide the remaining batter amongst the tins, being careful to seal in the sauce.

5 Place the puddings directly into the air fryer basket, and bake for 16–18 minutes until the sponge is golden and firm, but with a slight wobble.

6 Leave to cool for a few minutes before flipping out onto plates. Serve with salted caramel ice cream.

**Prep + cook time
50 minutes
Makes 4**

BANANA GALETTE

WITH CHOCOLATE FUDGE SAUCE

120g (1 stick) unsalted butter, softened
80g (generous ½ cup) icing
   (confectioners') sugar
1 large (US extra large) egg, beaten
½ tsp vanilla paste
½ tsp salt
200g (1½ cups) plain (all-purpose)
   flour, plus extra for dusting
3 small ripe bananas, peeled
1 egg, beaten
to serve: ice cream

FRANGIPANE:
50g (3½ tbsp) unsalted butter, softened
50g (¼ cup) golden caster
   (superfine) sugar
80g (¾ cup) ground hazelnuts
1 large (US extra large) egg
2 tbsp unsweetened cocoa powder
2 tbsp plain (all-purpose) flour

SAUCE:
400g (14oz) can condensed milk
20g (1½ tbsp) unsalted butter
100g (3½oz) dark (bittersweet)
   chocolate
2 tbsp unsweetened cocoa powder,
   plus extra to serve
1 tsp vanilla paste

1 Combine the butter with the icing sugar in a mixing bowl and beat until light. Stir in the beaten egg, vanilla, and salt, then fold through the flour until you have a stiff dough.
2 Form the dough into a ball and flatten into a 2.5cm (1in) thick disc, wrap in clingfilm, and chill for 30 minutes in the fridge.
3 Meanwhile, make the frangipane. Combine the butter, sugar, and ground hazelnuts in a bowl. Beat in the egg, then sift in the cocoa and flour. Fold through until combined.
4 On a floured surface, roll out the pastry into a 30cm (12in) circle. Place on a piece of baking parchment on a baking tray.
5 Spread the frangipane in the centre of the circle, leaving a 5cm (2in) border around the edge. Halve the bananas lengthways and place on the frangipane, pushing them in so the frangipane comes up around the fruit.

6 Fold the edges of the pastry into the centre, cover in clingfilm, and place in the fridge to chill for at least 30 minutes (and up to overnight).
7 Once chilled, brush the edges of the pastry with beaten egg. Trim any excess baking paper so you have just enough to be able to lift the tart in and out of the basket.
8 Preheat the air fryer to 180°C/350°F for 3 minutes.
9 Place in the air fryer basket and cook at 180°C/350°F for 35 minutes.
10 Meanwhile, combine all the sauce ingredients in a small pan over a low heat and stir until melted.
11 Let the galette cool in the basket for 20 minutes, before sliding out. Serve with the warm chocolate sauce, ice cream, and a dusting of cocoa powder.

Prep + cook time
**1 hour 30 minutes,
plus chilling
Serves 8**

CHERRY & RICOTTA CRUMBLE

400g (14oz) frozen cherries
150g (¾ cup) golden caster
   (superfine) sugar
juice of 1 lemon
2 tbsp brandy or liquor of choice
   (optional)
3 tsp cornflour (cornstarch)
100g (scant ½ cup) ricotta
to serve: store-bought custard

CRUMBLE:
60g (½ stick) butter, cubed and cold
100g (¾ cup) wholemeal
   (wholewheat) flour
50g (¼ cup) soft light brown sugar
50g (generous ⅓ cup) hazelnuts,
   roughly chopped
1 tsp flaked sea salt

1 Preheat the air fryer to 180°C/350°F for 3 minutes.

2 Combine the cherries, sugar, lemon juice, brandy (if using), and cornflour in a bowl, stirring until the cornflour has dissolved. Pour into a 20cm (8in) heatproof dish.

3 Bake at 180°C/350°F for 20 minutes, stirring halfway through. If the cherry filling is liquidy, place back in the air fryer at 200°C/400°F for 5 minutes (this will help activate the cornflour).

4 Meanwhile, make the crumble. Place the cold cubed butter and flour in a mixing bowl, and, using your fingertips, rub the butter into the flour until it resembles coarse sand. Stir through the sugar, hazelnuts, and salt.

5 Remove the heatproof dish from the air fryer, dollop the ricotta all over using a small spoon, then cover the top with the crumble. Place back in the air fryer basket and bake for a further 25 minutes at 180°C/350°F, or until the crumble is golden and the filling is bubbling up through the edges.

6 Leave to cool for 10–15 minutes before serving with custard.

KEEP IT This will keep for up to 3 days in an airtight container in the fridge.

Prep + cook time
1 hour 30 minutes
Serves 6

RHUBARB & GINGER COBBLER (VEGAN)

600g (1lb 5oz) rhubarb
65g (2¼oz) stem ginger in syrup, chopped, plus 2 tbsp of the syrup
125g (½ cup plus 2 tbsp) light soft brown sugar
grated zest and juice of 1 lemon
1½ tsp cornflour (cornstarch)
to serve: plant-based custard

COBBLER TOPPING:
70g (2½oz) dairy-free butter, softened
70g (6 tbsp) golden caster (superfine) sugar
125g (scant 1 cup) plain (all-purpose) flour
½ tsp salt
½ tsp baking powder
60ml (¼ cup) plant-based milk
1 tsp vanilla paste

1 Preheat the air fryer to 180°C/350°F for 3 minutes.
2 Trim the rhubarb and cut into 2.5cm (1in) chunks. Combine in a mixing bowl with the chopped ginger, sugar, lemon juice and zest, and cornflour. Give the mixture a good stir, then pour into a 22cm (9in) heatproof dish.
3 Roast for 15 minutes at 180°C/350°F, stirring every 5 minutes.
4 Meanwhile, make the cobbler topping. Combine the butter and sugar in a large mixing bowl and beat for 2 minutes, then add all the remaining ingredients and mix until you have a smooth but thick batter.
5 Remove the compote from the air fryer and dollop the cobbler on top.

6 Place straight back in the air fryer to bake for 18–20 minutes, or until the top is golden and the compote is bubbling through the gaps.
7 Leave to cool for 10 minutes before serving with plant-based custard.

KEEP IT Will keep for up to 5 days in an airtight container in the fridge.

**Prep + cook time
50 minutes
Serves 4–6**

MINI MERINGUE SUNDAES

150ml (⅔ cup) double (heavy) cream
1 tsp vanilla paste
100g (3½oz) raspberries
4–6 scoops of raspberry sorbet
pulp of 2 passion fruits
4–6 tbsp white chocolate sauce
2–4 tbsp chopped nuts

MERINGUE:
2 egg whites
½ tsp white wine vinegar
½ tsp cornflour (cornstarch)
120g (½ cup plus 2 tbsp) caster
  (superfine) sugar
2–3 drops pink food colouring
  (optional)

1 Start by making the meringue. Place the egg whites in a large mixing bowl. Using a hand-held electric whisk, mix the egg whites on medium speed until frothy and doubled in size. Add the white wine vinegar and cornflour, and whisk for 30 seconds. Now, gradually add the caster sugar, a dessert spoon at a time. Keep whisking until all the sugar is combined and the mixture is thick and glossy. Whisk in the food colouring, if using.

2 Preheat the air fryer to 120°C/250°F for 3 minutes.

3 Cut a piece of baking parchment to fit the air fryer basket. Use a little dab of meringue to stick each corner of the paper down to the basket. Using a teaspoon, place dollops of meringue into the basket. They will puff up and double in size, so leave a 2.5cm (1in) gap between them.

4 Bake at 120°C/250°F for 20 minutes, in batches, until all the meringue is used. Leave to cool on a wire rack.

5 To assemble the sundaes, whip the double cream with the vanilla paste to soft peaks. In sundae glasses, layer the whipped cream, meringues, berries, and a scoop of sorbet, then top with more cream, berries, and meringue. Finish with passion fruit pulp, chocolate sauce, and chopped nuts.

KEEP IT Extra meringues can be kept in an airtight container for up to 5 days.

**Prep + cook time
1 hour
Makes 4–6
(24 mini meringues)**

CHOCOLATE PAVLOVA

300ml (1¼ cups) double (heavy)
   cream
1 tbsp icing (confectioners') sugar
1 tsp vanilla paste
4 tbsp salted caramel sauce
to decorate: chocolates, honeycomb,
   and chocolate curls

MERINGUE:
4 egg whites
1 tsp white wine vinegar
1 tsp cornflour (cornstarch)
240g (scant 1¼ cups) caster
   (superfine) sugar
2 tbsp unsweetened cocoa powder

1 Start by making the meringue. Place the egg whites in a large mixing bowl. Using a hand-held electric whisk, mix the egg whites on medium speed until frothy and doubled in size. Add the white wine vinegar and cornflour, and whisk again for 30 seconds. Now, gradually add the caster sugar, a dessert spoon at a time. Keep whisking until all the sugar is combined and the mixture is thick and glossy.

2 Put half of the meringue in another bowl and sift in the cocoa powder. Fold through gently – it doesn't need to be fully combined, just swirled.

3 In a base-lined 20cm (8in) loose-bottomed round tin, alternate spoonfuls of plain meringue and cocoa meringue. Using a spoon, swirl the mixes together. Using the back of a spoon, create a dip in the centre for the cream and toppings to sit once baked.

4 Preheat the air fryer to 120°C/250°F for 3 minutes.

5 Place the pavlova in the preheated air fryer basket and bake at 120°C/250°F for 40 minutes, then turn down the air fryer to 100°C/200°F and bake for a further 30 minutes.

6 Leave the meringue to cool completely in the tin on a wire rack before gently removing it from the tin and placing it on a serving plate.

7 Whip the double cream with the icing sugar and vanilla to soft peaks, then spoon over the centre of the pavlova. Drizzle over the salted caramel, arrange the chocolates on top, and serve!

KEEP IT Will keep in the fridge for up to 3 days in an airtight container.

**Prep + cook time
2 hours
Serves 6–8**

PINEAPPLE FRITTERS WITH RUM CARAMEL SAUCE

50g (½ cup) cornflour (cornstarch)
70g (½ cup) plain (all-purpose) flour
35g (½ cup) desiccated (dried
   unsweetened shredded) coconut
120ml (½ cup) sparkling water
2 tbsp caster (superfine) sugar
1 pineapple, trimmed and cut
   into batons
vegetable oil cooking spray
to serve: toasted coconut

RUM CARAMEL SAUCE:
200g (1 cup) caster (superfine) sugar
120ml (½ cup) double (heavy) cream
40g (3 tbsp) unsalted butter
2 tbsp rum
1 tsp flaked sea salt

1 First, make the rum caramel sauce. Place the caster sugar in a wide heavy-based pan and add 3 tablespoons water around the edge of the pan. Place on a medium heat and, as the sugar starts to melt, swirl the pan. Do not stir the sugar, as it can cause sugar crystals to form resulting in a lumpy caramel. Keep swirling the pan until the sugar turns a deep golden brown; it will be bubbling and starting to gently smoke.

2 At this point, turn off the heat and pour the cream into the pan, being careful as the caramel will bubble and spit. Once the mixture has calmed slightly, swirl the pan again, then add the butter, rum, and sea salt. Use a whisk to combine. Leave the caramel to cool in the pan for 10–15 minutes before pouring into a heatproof container. Set aside.

3 Whisk the cornflour, plain flour, desiccated coconut, sparkling water, and sugar in a mixing bowl until all the flour is absorbed.

4 Preheat the air fryer to 200°C/400°F for 3 minutes and line an air fryer basket with greaseproof paper.

5 Toss chunks of pineapple in the batter to coat on all sides. Using tongs, lift the slices of pineapple into the lined air fryer basket, leaving 5cm (2in) between each piece.

6 Bake at 200°C/400°F for 8 minutes, then spray with oil and bake for a further 2–4 minutes until starting to golden.

7 Remove the fritters from the basket and coat in the rum caramel.

8 Place on a serving platter, sprinkle with toasted coconut, and serve with extra caramel sauce.

Prep + cook time
45 minutes
Serves 6

BAKED PEACHES
(VEGAN)

4 firm-but-ripe peaches, stoned (pitted) and halved
juice of 1 lemon
1 tsp vanilla paste
2 tbsp golden caster (superfine) sugar
to serve: plant-based custard

CRUMBLE TOP:
30g (1oz) dairy-free butter, cold and cubed
60g (scant ½ cup) plain (all-purpose) flour
30g (2½ tbsp) Demerara (raw) sugar
20g (¼ cup) flaked (slivered) almonds
1 tsp flaked sea salt

1 Preheat the air fryer to 180°C/350°F for 3 minutes.

2 Place the halved peaches in a 20cm (8in) heatproof dish, cut-side up, and squeeze over the lemon juice. Add the vanilla paste and sugar, and mix to coat. Place in the air fryer basket and bake for 5 minutes at 180°C/350°F.

3 To make the crumble, place the cold cubed butter in a small bowl with the plain flour, and rub the butter into the flour using your fingertips until it resembles coarse sand. Stir through the sugar, almonds, and sea salt.

4 Cover the peaches with mounds of the crumble (don't worry if it falls off the peaches into the dish, these bits will caramelize and can be scooped out).

5 Bake for a further 10 minutes at 180°C/350°F, or until the crumble is golden and the peaches are soft.

6 Serve warm with custard and any bits of crumble from the air fryer basket.

KEEP IT Can be kept for up to 5 days in an airtight container in the fridge.

**Prep + cook time
30 minutes
Serves 4**

VANILLA RICE PUDDING

100g (generous ½ cup) jasmine or
   pudding rice
500ml (2 cups) full-fat (whole) milk
60g (5 tbsp) light soft brown sugar
1 tsp vanilla paste
½ tsp fine salt
200ml (scant 1 cup) double (heavy)
   cream
to serve: raspberry jam,
   nut butter, and cold cream

1 Preheat the air fryer
to 160°C/325°F for
3 minutes.
2 Combine all the rice
pudding ingredients apart
from the double cream in a
20cm (8in) heatproof dish.
3 Place in the air fryer
basket and bake for
30 minutes, stirring every
10 minutes to ensure even
cooking. The rice should be
tender, but still have a little
bite to it; taste the rice at
each 10-minute interval
and amend the cooking
time to suit your preferred
level of bite.

4 Once the rice is cooked,
all the milk has been
absorbed, and it has a silky
consistency, remove the
dish from the air fryer and
stir through the cream.
5 Serve warm with
raspberry jam, nut butter,
and extra old cream.

KEEP IT Can be chilled
and eaten cold. Keep
for up to 3 days in an
airtight container.

**Prep + cook time
45 minutes
Serves 2–4**

APPLE HOT CROSS BUN PUDDING

150ml (⅔ cup) full-fat (whole) milk
75ml (⅓ cup) double (heavy) cream
60g (5 tbsp) golden caster
   (superfine) sugar
1 tsp vanilla extract
1 egg
4 hot cross buns
50g (3½ tbsp) salted butter
2 tbsp Demerara (raw) sugar

COMPOTE:
3 eating apples, peeled and chopped
50g (⅓ cup) jumbo raisins
30g (2½ tbsp) golden caster
   (superfine) sugar
20g (1½ tbsp) salted butter
juice of ½ lemon
1 tsp ground cinnamon

1 Preheat the air fryer to 160°C/325°F for 3 minutes.

2 Start by making the compote. Combine the chopped apples with the raisins, sugar, butter, and lemon juice in a 20cm (8in) round heatproof dish.

3 Place in the air fryer and bake for 15 minutes at 160°C/325°F, checking at 5-minute intervals and giving the apples a good mix each time. Once baked, set aside to cool.

4 In a large measuring jug (cup), measure out the milk and cream, then combine with the caster sugar, vanilla, and egg. Whisk thoroughly until you have a smooth custard-like liquid.

5 Cut the hot cross buns in half, and butter the cut side generously. Place one piece of bun in the ovenproof dish, followed by a spoonful of the apple compote and repeat until all the mix is used.

6 Pour the custard mix gently all over (you may need to wait for it to soak in a little before pouring it all in). You can use the back of a spoon to press down the buns to help make space for all the filling.

7 Preheat the air fryer to 180°C/350°F for 3 minutes.

8 Sprinkle the top of the pudding with the Demerara sugar, then place in the air fryer and cook at 180°C/350°F for 25 minutes until puffed up with a deep golden crust.

SERVE IT Serve warm with cream or a scoop of ice cream.

KEEP IT Can be kept for up to 3 days in an airtight container in the fridge.

Prep + cook time
1 hour
Serves 6

DUTCH BABY WITH BLUEBERRY COMPOTE

70g (½ cup) plain (all-purpose) flour
½ tsp salt
¼ tsp baking powder
2 tsp caster (superfine) sugar
80ml (⅓ cup) milk
2 eggs, beaten
½ tsp vanilla extract
20ml (4 tsp) vegetable oil
to serve: ice cream and icing
  (confectioners') sugar

BLUEBERRY COMPOTE:
200g (1½ cups) blueberries
50g (¼ cup) caster (superfine) sugar
grated zest and juice of 1 lemon

1 Place the flour, salt, baking powder, and sugar in a mixing bowl. Make a well in the middle, then add the milk, eggs, and vanilla, and whisk until smooth. Set aside for 20 minutes to rest.

2 Preheat the air fryer to 180°C/350°F for 3 minutes.

3 Put all the blueberry compote ingredients in a heatproof dish and place in the air fryer for 10 minutes at 180°C/350°F. Remove and set aside.

4 Increase the temperature to 200°C/400°F.

5 Put the vegetable oil in an 18cm (7in) round pie dish or cake tin, and heat in the air fryer at 200°C/400°F for 3 minutes. The oil needs to be smoking hot, so take care and do not try to lift the dish out of the basket at this point.

6 Pour the batter directly into the hot oil, then bake for 12 minutes at 200°C/400°F.

7 Using tongs, lift the (now inflated) pudding and flip it upside down, then bake for a further 8 minutes to crisp the bottom.

8 Serve straight away while hot, topped with the blueberry compote and ice cream, and dusted with icing sugar.

Prep + cook time
50 minutes
Serves 4–6

CONVERSION CHART

DRY MEASURES

metric	imperial
15g	½oz
30g	1oz
60g	2oz
90g	3oz
125g	4oz (¼lb)
155g	5oz
185g	6oz
220g	7oz
250g	8oz (½lb)
280g	9oz
315g	10oz
345g	11oz
375g	12oz (¾lb)
410g	13oz
440g	14oz
470g	15oz
500g	16oz (1lb)
750g	24oz (1½lb)
1kg	32oz (2lb)

OVEN TEMPERATURES

The oven temperatures below are for conventional ovens; if you are using a fan-forced oven, reduce the temperature by 20 degrees.

	°C (Celsius)	°F (Fahrenheit)
Very slow	120	250
Slow	150	300
Moderately slow	160	325
Moderate	180	350
Moderately hot	200	400
Hot	220	425
Very hot	240	475

LIQUID MEASURES

metric	imperial
30ml	1 fluid oz
60ml	2 fluid oz
100ml	3 fluid oz
125ml	4 fluid oz
150ml	5 fluid oz
190ml	6 fluid oz
250ml	8 fluid oz
300ml	10 fluid oz
500ml	16 fluid oz
600ml	20 fluid oz
1000ml (1 litre)	1¾ pints

LENGTH MEASURES

metric	imperial
3mm	⅛in
6mm	¼in
1cm	½in
2cm	¾in
2.5cm	1in
5cm	2in
6cm	2½in
8cm	3in
10cm	4in
13cm	5in
15cm	6in
18cm	7in
20cm	8in
22cm	9in
25cm	10in
28cm	11in
30cm	12in (1ft)

One Australian metric tablespoon holds 20ml; one Australian metric teaspoon holds 5ml. North America, New Zealand and the United Kingdom use a 15ml tablespoon. The most accurate way of measuring dry ingredients is to weigh them.

INDEX

DK LONDON

Project Editor Izzy Holton
Senior Designer Tania Gomes
Senior Production Editor David Almond
Senior Production Controller Stephanie McConnell
Sales and Jackets Co-ordinator Emily Cannings
Editorial Director Cara Armstrong
Art Director Maxine Pedliham

Recipe development Lucy Turnbull
Editorial Kate Reeves-Brown
Food styling Lucy Turnbull
Food styling assistants Kristine Jakobson,
Immy Mucklow
Prop styling Hannah Wilkinson
Photographer Tony Briscoe

DK DELHI

Managing Art Editor Neha Ahuja
DTP Coordinator Pushpak Tyagi
DTP Designers Raman Panwar, Satish Gaur
Pre-production Manager Balwant Singh

First published in Great Britain in 2024 by
Dorling Kindersley Limited
20 Vauxhall Bridge Road, London SW1V 2SA

The authorized representative in the EEA is
Dorling Kindersley Verlag GmbH. Arnulfstr. 124,
80636 Munich, Germany

Copyright © 2024 Dorling Kindersley Limited
A Penguin Random House Company
10 9 8 7 6 5 4 3 2 1
001–345958–Oct/2024

All rights reserved.
No part of this publication may be reproduced, stored
in or introduced into a retrieval system, or transmitted,
in any form, or by any means (electronic, mechanical,
photocopying, recording, or otherwise), without the
prior written permission of the copyright owner.

A CIP catalogue record for this book
is available from the British Library.
ISBN: 978-0-2417-2743-0

Printed and bound in the United Kingdom

www.dk.com

PUBLISHER ACKNOWLEDGMENTS

DK would like to thank Lucy Turnbull for recipe
development, Kathy Steer for proofreading,
and Lisa Footitt for indexing.

MIX
Paper | Supporting
responsible forestry
FSC™ C018179

This book was made with Forest
Stewardship Council™ certified
paper – one small step in DK's
commitment to a sustainable future.
Learn more at www.dk.com/uk/
information/sustainability